Church Officers at Work

By

GLENN H. ASQUITH

JUDSON PRESS
VALLEY FORGE

Except where otherwise indicated, the Bible quotations in this volume
are in accordance with the Revised Standard Version of the Bible, copy-
right 1946 and 1952 by the Division of Christian Education of the
National Council of the Churches of Christ in the United States of
America, and are used by permission.

Second Edition (Revised), 1952
Third Printing, June, 1954
Fourth Printing, June, 1956
Fifth Printing, November, 1958
Sixth Printing, December, 1961
Seventh Printing (Revised), July, 1963
Eighth Printing, September, 1965
Ninth Printing, April, 1967
Tenth Printing, July, 1969
Eleventh Printing, December, 1970
Twelfth Printing, March, 1972

Text approved for Administration Course 612a
by the Leadership Education Department
of the American Baptist Board of Education
and Publication.

International Standard Book No. 0-8170-0048-8

Contents

Concerning the Author

Rev. Glenn H. Asquith, D.D., received his formal education in the public schools of Rochester, N.Y., and at the Eastern Baptist College (B.A.) and the Eastern Baptist Theological Seminary (Th.B.). In 1952 that seminary conferred on him the honorary degree of Doctor of Divinity.

He has had five important and successful pastorates: First Church, Manayunk, Philadelphia; First Church, Salem, N. J.; First Church, Westerly, R. I.; Asylum Avenue, Hartford, Conn.; First United Baptist Church, Lowell, Mass.; and First Baptist Church, Montclair, New Jersey.

From 1950 to 1956 he was Executive Secretary of the New York State Baptist Convention. He served on numerous boards and committees, some denominational, some interdenominational.

From 1960 to 1961 he was Executive Secretary of the Philadelphia Baptist Association.

He was Executive Director of the Division of Christian Publications, American Baptist Board of Education and Publication, from 1961 to 1967.

An author of many widely read articles, tracts, and books, *A Two-Century Church, Lively May I Walk, Selected Works of Ryters Krampe* and *Cousin Tom,* he has also received a Freedoms Foundation (Valley Forge) Award and other literary recognitions. His experience as a pastor and later as a denominational secretary gives him an understanding of the needs of churches; therefore, he is well qualified to discuss in practical, down-to-earth fashion the duties of the various church officers and the functions of the church's several boards and committees.

Introduction

THIS book attempts to delineate the work of church officers and to suggest how their work might be carried out effectively. The Department of Leadership Education of the American Baptist Convention commissioned the writing of *Church Officers at Work* to serve as a text for a leadership education course. The writer was reminded of the description of this administration course (in a then-current educational bulletin) and was given this as a focus:

> "Many times the members of the different official bodies of the church raise questions as to the exact responsibility in the total work of the church which each should be carrying; as to the relationship between the various official boards; as to the way in which these boards should work together in developing a single program for the church; as to the functions of the church and the purposes and functions of its various organizations; as to the work of officers in the local church in relationship to the work of the denomination. Taking into account the polity of the particular church to which members of the class belong, this course should attempt to answer such questions as these, as the members of the class face the total task of their churches and their responsibilities as officials."

Primarily, the purpose of this book is to meet such needs expressed by pastors and other church officers. A second purpose is to serve as a textbook in classes and schools, with particular emphasis on the organization of a Baptist church. Beyond this, however, the writer hopes that the book will be helpful to pastors and laymen of churches of all denominations.

—GLENN H. ASQUITH

July, 1963

*A*ND his gifts were that some should be apostles, some prophets, some evangelists, some pastors and teachers, for the equipment of the saints, for the work of ministry, for building up the body of Christ.

—EPHESIANS 4:11-12

CHAPTER I

The Basis of the Work

WHAT OFFICERS did the first church in Jerusalem have, and what were their duties? If we go back no further than Pentecost to locate the first New Testament church, the group which gathered together following the inspired preaching of Peter and his companions on that wondrous day described in Acts 2, we shall find that there were no officers except the preacher for the day, and no duties. Here we have the reason for the lack of organization—no duties. Where there is nothing to be done, officials are not needed. That first church had no roll of members, with names and street addresses to be kept up to date, no bank account to be kept balanced, no bills to pay, no building to be maintained. As the months and years went on, of course, that church found one problem of administration after another, and each had to be solved. One by one church offices were created to meet the needs as they arose. This also is the basis accepted by Baptist churches today, the need coupled with the simplest and most efficient way of caring for it.

I. Polity and Practice

"Polity" is a word which is rarely used by the average man of today, but it persists in church documents. It is derived from a Greek word meaning "government," and it has come to mean the form of government of a church. We can think of the polity of our church as the recognized principles underlying the working of the church. It is the unwritten constitution and by-laws against which all action is tested. There are two types of church polity to be found among denominations today, episcopal and congregational. There are shades and variations, but, in the large, a church will subscribe to one or the other of these. The episcopal type is authoritarian, with final decisions vested in a hierarchy of bishops of varying degrees and designated by a variety of titles. Congregational polity is democratic in the sense that final decisions are vested

7

in the membership of the church. It is this polity which Baptist churches hold as their New Testament birthright and which will be discussed here.

To understand Baptist church polity it will be necessary to go back to the beginnings. The primary tenet of Baptist churches is that the New Testament is the sufficient and only acceptable rule of faith and order. Whatever is found in the New Testament, then, in reference to church government will be received in preference to other historical precedent, expediency, or ecclesiastical dicta. And this is found: constant testimony to the competency of the church. Any group of believers coming together regularly for worship may be honored with the name "church." Like the apostles, members defer to the church's voice in the matters of setting apart men for the ministry, the choice of deacons, and voluntary offerings for the needy in other places. This privilege of the church we call "autonomy," the right of self-government.

Autonomy works out with great similarity in the churches despite the freedom involved. Starting from the same principle, most churches come out at the same destination of self-imposed rules and of self-set standards of achievement, although the routes may not exactly correspond. The progress of a new church along this road will best illustrate our polity in action.

II. Organizing a Church

Let us think of a Baptist family moving into a new town. On Sunday morning this family looks about for a church and finds none. As the days go on, the father and mother meet men and women who are looking for a Christian church and especially for a Sunday church school for themselves and their children. Someone suggests the advisability of getting together to discuss the matter of a church, but not all are Baptists. What should they do? Start several competitive, struggling groups or seek a way out together without anyone foregoing his religious convictions? A call to the state convention secretary will bring help. In fact, it is quite possible that he has been working with representatives of other denominations to discover how the new housing area can be served best by the denominations.

It may be that through co-operation between the people in the housing area and the Baptist state convention a plan for a community Baptist church may be arranged, each family thus receiving the best leadership possible because all agree to share in an adequate ministry. Under other circumstances, it may be true that a group of Baptists is strong enough to initiate plans for a Baptist church. In this day of desperate need to serve so many with a more effective program, few Christians have a taste for competitive Christianity. Every group will have to determine its own procedure, however. A meeting is called and, in due time, a group gathers, selects a moderator, and proceeds with the business of the meeting. As soon as the moderator is elected, he will take charge and call for the election of a clerk, or secretary.

If, in the following discussion, it is agreed to organize a Baptist church, the group will elect or appoint a committee on the constitution and set a date for the next meeting at which this committee is to report. Adjournment of the first meeting will be by common consent.

The committee on the constitution will now start work. Probably they will borrow copies of the constitutions of their home churches; they may obtain samples of model constitutions from the state office. Using these as guides only, they will prepare a constitution which they think is adapted to the needs of the new church in the new community. They will realize that their work may be changed, for the next meeting may revise their document. This is a hazard which every committee must face. Rarely is such a committee appointed "with power."

At the next meeting, after the moderator has declared that a report of the committee is in order, a free and frank discussion will be held. In all likelihood many of the articles in the proposed constitution will be changed, and some may be added. The constitution will set forth: the purpose of organization; the name of the church; the officers and committees to be elected with their responsibilities and duties; an article of rules concerning membership; the time and place of meetings; and the financial status. After the adoption of the constitution and the election of the officers named in it, the group is, essentially, a Baptist church. In some states, the church will not be recognized legally until the clerk has filed a copy of the constitution with the Secretary of State, together with a petition for a charter to be granted by the State Legislature. If all is in order, this charter would be granted at the next session of the legislature.

Locally and legally the church is now a church. Even though the majority favored remaining independent of all Baptist ties, that would not forfeit the title "Baptist." The sense of fellowship and responsibility is so strong in most churches, however, that the vote is likely to be for membership in some association. A petition for membership and recognition will be sent to the chosen association. If the other churches in the association vote favorably on the application, a service of recognition for the new church will be planned. If the Association is affiliated with a state convention, and it in turn is affiliated with the American Baptist Convention, the new church automatically becomes related to these larger groups unless its members take formal action otherwise.

There remains only the calling of a pastor, and the new church will be ready to function as a Baptist church on a par with other autonomous churches. All actions will be based on the same polity which enabled the church voluntarily to bring itself into being, and it will remain in existence so long as there are members and can go out of existence only by the voluntary consent of a majority.

III. A Church's Relationships

The organization of one church is essentially the same as that of every other Baptist church in the world. Organization, association, administration, and activities are purely voluntary and autonomous.

1. *The Association.* Fellowship and co-operation with other Baptist churches is a part of the life of the church. Such relationships are established and maintained by voluntary association, as a right of autonomous groups.

The pastor and a certain number of men and women are elected by the church to be delegates. They attend the association meetings and present a report of the work during the year. Statistics are presented to the clerk who compiles a report of accessions, losses, Sunday church school data, and such other information as the association believes important. Any one who has tried to write the history of a church or to establish facts about members of churches knows how important these data are. The cost of reports and other incidental expenses is paid from the income received as dues from churches.

Associations have no power over Baptist churches. They are the churches in co-operation. Some associations are more active than others. In a few states, a group of associations carry on their own missionary activities together and sponsor evangelistic, stewardship, and Christian education programs as well as social righteousness crusades on the association level.

The importance of the association as a powerful link between neighboring churches has decreased as means of transportation and communication have improved. Today, a state convention is almost as accessible to a church as once an association was. Churches continue to gather as members of an association; however, unless they choose otherwise, they are considered to be members of the State Convention. This unit is the active missionary unit in most areas.

2. *The State Convention.* A state convention is the churches of the area in voluntary co-operation, usually for the purpose of strengthening the churches through special services, administering missionary work on behalf of the churches, collecting the funds administered by the state, and co-operating with the national convention in promoting the giving of funds for the World Mission Budget (the unified budget of the American Baptist Convention).

In a number of states, in addition to the Executive Secretary (who frequently serves also as Director of Promotion), there are other staff members: Director of Evangelism, Director of Christian Education, Director of Town and Country Work, Area Representatives, and others. Each state establishes its own staff according to its needs and its financial ability. Often national organizations co-operate in some of the salaries or in travel expense for secretaries. For one thing, these state workers are available to help the small church plan programs and train lay workers, thus assisting the pastor and providing trained diversified supplementary leadership.

3. *The City Society.* Certain cities across the United States are so large and have such heavy administrative responsibility for missionary work and community activities that they are organized for work in a manner similar to state conventions. Churches in such areas may find that their Association is called a City Society; their membership is in this group, although they

are usually related to the State Convention as well.

4. *The American Baptist Convention.* The church has one more link that relates it directly to the whole World Mission of Baptists. The American Baptist Convention is successor to a line of agencies organized to carry forward missionary activities, and is direct successor to the Northern Baptist Convention which took the name, American Baptist Convention, at the annual meeting in Boston in May, 1950. There are numerous other Baptist conventions in the United States. Besides the less known bilingual conventions and about 175 small groups of Baptists recognized in the Religious Census, there are the Southern Baptist Convention—the largest, the National Baptist Convention in the United States of America, the National Baptist Convention of America, and the Progressive National Baptist Convention. All of these are made up of Baptist churches in voluntary co-operation.

In the American Baptist Convention the voluntary relationship is very strong. The raising of the great World Mission budget each year is the responsibility of the convention's Division of World Mission Support, but it is the hearty participation of each church that brings the goal in sight.

The mission societies, publishing board, and other agencies of the American Baptist Convention are made up of persons who come from Baptist churches, and each agency reports to the churches at the national convention. Its annual report appears in the Year Book of the American Baptist Convention.

All of this activity in the association and in state and national conventions is the work of local churches in free co-operation. Baptist churches have found that "in union there is strength," while they have retained their belief in a complete democracy.

5. *Councils of Churches.* Through the national convention and also by direct action, a Baptist church may accept a share in the great interdenominational task, locally and in its world-wide aspects. A church finds financial and service obligations in such relationships, but the church is enriched by the responsibilities.

IV. Structural Organization

Democracy in a church or in a nation does not imply haphazardness or deny authority. The systematic procedures, however, are instituted and maintained by democratic action, and the authority is self-imposed. The voting membership in a Baptist church is, and must always be, the body of final reference and the holder of the veto power. Voting membership is the term used in order to distinguish between regular membership and associate membership which is practiced in some churches. In most churches having this dual membership plan, associate members are limited in voting privileges.

If we separate our church-governing bodies into three branches such as we find in the federal government of the United States, we shall find that the voting membership conforms to the legislative branch.

EXECUTIVE	*LEGISLATIVE*	*JUDICIAL*
The Staff:	*The Church*	*Advisory Council*
Pastor, etc.	Voting Membership	

1. *Legislative branch.* The voting membership, the legislative branch of the church government, meets in accordance with the provisions of the constitution adopted at the time of the organization of the church. An annual meeting is held in all Baptist churches, and semiannual, quarterly, or even monthly meetings are the rule in some churches. In addition to these regular meetings, all churches make provision for special and emergency meetings. It is a rare church which can nurture its democratic character and go through a full year, from annual meeting to annual meeting, without the necessity for special meetings to decide some urgent questions. The privileges and responsibilities of the voting membership are many.

(a) No small job is the regulation of the voting membership itself. The constitution provides for admission and exclusion of members, and the church is bound by these provisions until it abrogates or amends them. The usual procedure is for the pastor to recommend the applicant to the board of deacons, after which the board of deacons will make a recommendation to the church.[1] The voting membership will then take whatever action it considers best. Requests for letters of transfer, and resignations, the matter of erasure of names of inactive members, and the exclusion of members for cause will go through the same procedure. This part of church business is very important, for the membership roll is the basis of all

---

[1] In this discussion, it is assumed that those who make application for membership in a Baptist church have accepted Jesus Christ as Lord and Savior and desire to enter the fellowship of the church by one of the approved methods for receiving members.

church activity and progress. The quality and amount of work done, the standing of a church in its community, and its future depend upon the members who make up the church. Carelessness in this part of the work results in a growing list of inactive and non-resident members.

(b) Second in importance to the control of the membership is the determining of the financial policy of the church. Very little can be done by elected or appointed officials without an appropriation of money. The power of a budget carefully drawn up, carefully balanced, and carefully adopted cannot be overestimated. When a member votes for a suggested budget, he is expressing his views on hundreds of issues which are automatically disposed of by the several appropriations. It is important that the items be examined and that the implications of the budget be understood since so much depends on its approval.

(c) Calling a pastor is another important duty of the voting membership. It is subordinated to the membership and financial actions chiefly because it is an infrequent item of business. However, when the need arises, the voting membership must vote for or against a candidate. Much of the responsibility for finding a pastor will be placed upon the shoulders of the pulpit committee that will be discussed later.

(d) The voting membership has another time-consuming task. The reports of boards and committees will come up for approval or ratification at the end of the church year. Important trends in church activity and thought are reflected in the annual reports of the various chairmen and other officials. The reports need to be checked against the authority which was granted at the time the committees were created and the officials elected, and progress should be noted with thanksgiving.

Beyond these privileges and prerogatives of the voting membership, most of the work is divided among committees and elected officials. A later chapter will deal with this part of the church program.

Thus the legislative branch of the local church government, the voting membership, charts the course for the church, elects officials, appoints committees, allocates the money, and holds the power of veto or censure for unauthorized actions of members or boards. We turn now to the executive branch.

2. *Executive branch.*

(*a*) The pastor, in some churches spoken of as the minister, heads up the staff which represents the executive branch of the church. He is responsible to the church as a whole for the conduct of his work, although some churches may have a committee on pastoral relations or pastoral service to make suggestion or offer criticism. Even so, the pastor, in a regular or special meeting, may appeal to the church if any decisions seem to him to be unfair or unwise.

A capable pastor who has been in a church long enough to gain the respect and confidence of his people often finds himself in the dangerous position of accepted dictator. Like George Washington, he may repeatedly refuse the crown without changing the fact in the hearts of many parishioners. The average member of a church has no skill or knowledge especially related to the conduct of a religious institution. He recognizes this fact and, at the same time, knows that his pastor has spent years in school learning how to lead a church and that his professional experience since graduation has made him efficient in the work. The member thinks of himself as being in the position of a stockholder of a telephone company. He cannot make minor repairs on his own home instrument, so why should he use his voting power to dictate the management of the corporation to men who have worked themselves up from the bottom of the ladder and who know the technical as well as the managerial details? As a consequence the member is inclined to "give the pastor what he wants."

(1) The pastor, then, usually initiates legislation. Beyond the routine business of church meetings, much of the discussion and action will be on matters of business suggested by the pastor. The church maintains its democratic character by restricting the pastor's power to his pastoral functions and by requiring that anything outside that field be submitted to the church. Even though the action may be in accordance with the best judgment of the pastor, nevertheless it is the church that makes the suggestion an act. Democratic procedures are slow, but they are surer and more satisfactory in the end. The executive branch of our national government recognizes this fact and so must the executive branch of a church.

(2) The larger share of the pastor's work is likely to be on the other side of the ledger. He will initiate much legislation, to be sure, but his principal task will be to carry out the purpose of the church as expressed in the constitution and by-laws, in the amendments, and in actions taken year by year. This work is summed up in the constitution of one church

in these words: "The Pastor shall preach, attend meetings of the advisory committee, and in general perform the duties common to pastors of Evangelical Churches." Not very definite, but just about as detailed as a similar clause in an average church constitution. The "duties common to pastors of evangelical churches" are all-inclusive. The pastor will be expected to preach, teach, call, perform marriage ceremonies, conduct funerals, represent the church at meetings of the association, state convention, and national convention, and make himself available for community projects. His will be the responsibility for organizing the work of the church, including the church school, and for keeping the organization running smoothly. His advice will be sought by the committees of the church and by the elected officials. He will be the promoter of special projects voted at church meetings. And, if there is a staff, he will be required to assemble the personnel and direct the work.

(3) The staff may include an assistant pastor or pastor's assistant, a director of Christian education, church secretary, director of music, superintendent of the building. Not many churches will have a full staff; indeed many will have no one but the pastor. However, in the discussion that follows, each of these positions will be treated separately, still recognizing that in many churches their work will be combined with that of others. The pastor will direct the staff by personal conference with the individual members and by regular staff meetings.

(*b*) The assistant pastor may be an ordained man or a student in a theological seminary. He is likely to be a young man gaining experience for a parish of his own, or an older man who has relinquished the heavier responsibilities of the pastorate. It is customary for the pastor to submit the name of his candidate to the pulpit committee, advisory committee, or other group responsible for oversight of this part of the work. Occasionally church action is required. An assistant pastor is responsible directly to the pastor and his duties will be determined by the pastor.

(*c*) The pastor's assistant may be a retired minister, a layman, or a woman with training or natural inclination for the work. The title "Church Visitor" is often used instead of pastor's assistant. Like the assistant pastor, this person is usually engaged by the pastor and responsible to him. His chief task will be parish calling. The assistant will follow up leads for prospective members and refer these to the pastor. Calls on each family on the church roll will enable the assistant to help the pastor keep in touch with homes.

(*d*) The director of Christian education holds a strategic position in a church and is engaged usually by the board of Christian education working with the pastor and advisory committee. Many churches require a church vote on his call. The director works with the pastor and must keep her work (the feminine pronoun is used due to the preponderance of women in this position) in harmony with his. The board of Christian education will meet with her regularly, and, sometimes, the board of deacons will review the work and make suggestions. Through the pastor or the board she may initiate legislation for church action.

The first responsibility of the director will be the conduct of a church school; the second task will be the co-ordination of all phases of Christian education in the church. Girl Scouts, Boy Scouts, vacation church school, children's activities, special programs for special days, picnics will be on her roster. She may plan a long-range program but should do so in consultation with the pastor and the board. The director's tenure of office is not necessarily dependent upon the pastor's stay in a church.

(*e*) The church secretary may be employed by the pastor. She will be responsible mainly to the pastor. Her qualifications will be more than the knowledge of shorthand and typing, for she will be called upon to act as a buffer between the parish and the members of the staff; to do work for many groups and organizations; and to plan the church calendar and other publicity. If full-time, she will be the only one spending the entire business day at the church; consequently, many decisions will devolve upon her. Tact is an asset of incalculable value in a church secretary.

(*f*) A director of music may or may not be the organist. Where there are two people sharing the work, the organist may or may not be counted a staff member. The work of these people will be discussed under the work of the music committee.

(*g*) The superintendent of the building, otherwise known as engineer, sexton, janitor, according to the size and location of the church, is engaged by and responsible to the board of trustees or building committee in consultation with the pastor. His is the job of keeping the church property clean and in good order. Any repairs which are beyond his skill he will call to the attention of the board. The lawns, including the trees and bushes, come under his supervision. He will be required to follow the schedule of church meetings, to make sure that the rooms are at the right temperature, and to have the doors unlocked at the specified times. He may have assistants to do the manual work while he acts as supervisor, or he may do all the work himself, depending on the size of the building. The changing of the letters in the outside bulletin boards may be within his jurisdiction. He must see that tables are set up for dinners, that the church is prepared for weddings, that the cards and pencils in pew racks are renewed regularly. The public will judge the church largely by the efficiency of the superintendent in keeping the appearance of the property worthy of the God to whom it is dedicated.

In a small church without a sexton it will relieve the pastor greatly if one of his members will assume responsibility for the heating and another for care of the grounds.

3. *Judicial branch.* In addition to the legislative group or voting membership of the church and the executive branch or the staff, there is the judicial branch of the church government, known as the advisory board.

(*a*) The advisory board varies as to membership, but usually a body of this kind is made up of all the officials of the church, plus the presidents of the societies, such as men's fellowship or club, woman's society, and youth fellowship. In addition, some churches elect from two to five members-at-large at their annual meeting. The aim is to obtain a complete representation of all activities within the church program. If this endeavor is successful, there will be no organized group within the church unaware of the plans and program of the whole church. The board will hold regular monthly meetings, with the possible exception of one or two summer months.

The board is an organized group, with a chairman and secretary selected at the first meeting following annual church elections. Some churches prefer that the pastor serve as permanent chairman, but this has the disadvantage of putting the minister in the middle of arguments. Too, the chairman is limited in the expression of opinion, but if the pastor sits as a member he is free to speak to any point that may arise.

The order of business at a regular meeting of the advisory board will include the following items, with local variations. The chairman will call the meeting to order. Prayer will be offered. The minutes will be read and corrected. The church treasurer's report of the month's financial transactions and the benevolence treasurer's report of his receipts and disbursements for the month will be received. The building committee will report on the condition of the property. Other necessary reports will be made, and then any old business picked up from the minutes will be disposed of or referred for later action. New business will occupy the remaining time.

(*b*) The nature of the business justifies the term "judicial branch." Any matter which an organization or individual proposes to bring before a church meeting ought to be cleared with the advisory board. This board is so representative as to protect the democratic right of all members of the church but is small enough to be efficient. The suggested item of business will be discussed with the view to determining whether or not it requires church action; it is possible that the board itself, or some other organization of the church, has jurisdiction and can act upon the matter. The items which are considered important enough to require church action will be referred to the clerk of the church for placing on the agenda of the next church meeting. If there is urgency, the advisory board will ask for a special meeting of the church. In the meantime, a subcommittee will be appointed by the board to gather the facts on the business to be presented to the church. This will save time and permit intelligent action.

(*c*) From the other direction, items of business passed by the church may need interpretation. There may be an uncertainty, for instance, as to the jurisdiction of the deacons and board of Christian education over some motion passed by the church. The advisory board will decide this and authorize the proper organization to carry out the church's instructions.

Many times the pastor will wish to present matters to the board before doing things out of the ordinary. The church may have suggested that a particular sermon of the pastor's be printed and distributed. Before using the money for this project, the pastor will prefer to have the recommendation of the board. By referring doubtful issues to the board, the pastor will protect himself from criticism and keep the church harmonious.

In churches which have an advisory board, the constitution will define the field of authority and, usually, give the board authority to act on all ordinary matters of business in the interim between regular meetings.

FOR STUDY AND DISCUSSION

1. After reading the account of the organization of churches in The Acts, what do you find to indicate that the early churches were (*a*) congregational or (*b*) episcopal in polity.
2. Compare the organization of your church with the material given under "Structural Organization." If major differences are noted, discuss the advantages and disadvantages of each method.
3. In your own situation, how does the division into legislative, executive, and judicial branches of church government apply?
4. Would a monthly meeting of the voting membership of the church be a good substitute for an advisory board? How is it done in your church?

PROJECTS FOR CLASS REPORT

1. Look up the report of the first meetings of your church, and summarize the various steps taken for organization.
2. Make a chart showing the officials, boards, committees, and organizations of your church, indicating the body or individual to which each is responsible.
3. Attend a meeting of the church, and make your own minutes for presentation to the class.

CLASS PROJECT

The class may follow the steps necessary to organize a church. A blackboard might be used to list the things done, and the officers and committees elected.

BIBLIOGRAPHY

Maring, Norman H., and Hudson, Winthrop S., *A Baptist Manual of Polity and Practice.*

Maring, Norman H., *American Baptists—Whence and Whither.*

McNutt, Wm. R., *Polity and Practice in Baptist Churches.*

Torbet, Robert G., *The Baptist Story.*

Vedder, H. C., *Short History of the Baptists.*

CHAPTER II

The Work of Committees

IN A CHURCH, no matter how small in membership, there are some tasks to be done which cannot be accomplished effectively in open meetings of the entire membership. Information must be secured, data assembled, and spade work done before the matter in hand can be presented to the church for intelligent action. Also there are items of business which are recurring throughout the year, and projects to be completed that call for special knowledge or ability. The efficient way to take care of these particular tasks is by committee action. A committee may consist of one or more members. The popular size of a committee is three or five.

Committees are subsidiary to the larger body which creates them. In a church there will be committees and sub-committees in every department of the work, but for the present we shall consider the major committees of the church. These are appointed in various ways. Nominations for membership on more important committees are brought before the annual meeting of the church and members are elected by ballot just as are the officers. Other committees are described in the constitution with the provision that the members be elected by the advisory board. And some committees are appointed by the moderator or chairman, with or without the ratification of the church.

After election or appointment of membership, a committee is organized. Usually the body creating the committee names the member who is to serve as chairman or proceeds on the assumption that the first-named member is to be chairman. Sometimes the member whose name heads the list is considered the convener to call the first meeting of the committee, at which time a permanent chairman is elected. It is customary to elect a secretary at the first meeting. Committees are obligated to report to the parent body according to their instructions. Some committees serve for a year, others until a specific task is completed, others until dismissed by the creating body. And with

21

this introduction we are ready to look more closely at some major church committees.

The Nominating Committee

Probably the most important and influential of all committees is the nominating committee; certainly this is true of the church. Despite the fact that church elections are democratic, the nominating committee practically selects the officers for the coming year. And the officers will lead the church to victory or failure, so the wisest men and women of a church are needed on this committee.

Due to the decisive character of its work, the nominating committee should be made up of not less than five members. If the church be large, a larger committee is indicated. Almost invariably, the chairman of this committee will be named by the church at the time the committee is created. Inasmuch as this committee affects directly the work of the church, it is a committee elected by the church gathered in annual meeting that serves through the next annual meeting. In brief, the work of this committee is to present to the church at the annual meeting a complete slate of officers and committee members to fill the vacancies occurring at the end of the current church year.

Elected at the annual meeting, and with a chairman designated, the nominating committee is ready to go to work. At the first meeting, of course, a secretary will be named, and the members will be cautioned to keep the work of the committee confidential. Working confidentially and quietly the committee will seek to do its work according to the powers granted to it. The first step will be to make a complete list of the offices to be filled. Not all of the officials of a church will go out of office after a one-year term. The list should include only the offices to be filled.

Taking the offices in turn, the committee will consider first the incumbent, the one who now holds the position. Churches have unwritten rules and traditions regarding certain offices. Some offices are understood to have a one-year term; others, such as the office of clerk and treasurer, are thought of as almost permanent. For the positions where there is no legal or traditional block to re-election, and where the official is giving good service and is willing to continue in office, the committee usually presents the name of the incumbent. If the committee feels that there is an outstanding reason for a change, perhaps to shift the official to a more important post, the official should be consulted. To omit the name of a faithful and willing servant without notification and explanation would be most unwise and disruptive.

For offices where re-election is not customary, the committee will first consider the next in line. It is not necessarily true that he is best fitted for the higher office, but he may well be. He will have had experience and training, and he may be expecting the promotion.

A third field that is a "must" for the committee's consideration includes officials who have been out of office long enough to have qualified again for election. For example: In some churches a man may serve as a deacon for three years and then be ineligible for re-election until he has been out of office for a full year. The same provisions are true of other offices, and the committee will be wise to consider these men who are in legal "exile."

After due consideration of the incumbents, the next in line, and the "exiles," the committee has a free hand. There will be a complete list of members of the church for consideration. Insofar as possible, the committee should assign the offices proportionately among members of long standing, new members, men, women, and young people. Members of long standing merit notice, but some new members ought to be included each year in order to utilize new talent and to dissipate the notion that "the same people run things all the time." It is essential, too, to give representation to the various age and sex groups. Women and young people are capable of serving the church officially as well as men.

When the committee has agreed upon a name for an office, some member of the committee should be appointed to speak to the candidate, outline simply and definitely the work of such office, and secure permission to have his name presented, explaining that this is in no wise a guarantee of election but merely a nomination. Until his permission is unequivocally granted, a man's name ought not to be presented.

When the nominating committee's report is called for at the annual meeting, the chairman or secretary will read it from a typed or carefully written copy. After reading, he will give the list to the clerk of the church.

If the nominating committee is elected annually, it is competent to care for any nominations which may arise during the year. Unless the constitution of the church states otherwise, the committee will present names for vacancies occurring during the year. If a new office or committee is created during the year, the committee will present a nomination for it.

Unless there is a by-law forbidding such action, the committee may bring in the name of one of its members for an office. In an efficient church, false modesty is a detriment to the work.

The Music Committee

The church and the nominating committee will do well to remember, when selecting the music committee, that the prime requisites for a capable member of this committee are: a knowledge of music, an appreciation of worship values, tact, and, if possible, no family relationship to the choir members. This is one of the committees elected at the annual meeting, usually for a one-year term. It should not be larger than five, and three would suffice.

The responsibility of the music committee concerns the entire music program of the church. It always should co-operate with the minister in planning this program. Ordinarily, the committee is qualified to serve during the year without referring to the church, just so long as it keeps within the budgetary allotment for music. In some churches, the hiring of a director of music requires the ratification of the church. The director of music, the organist, the paid members of the choir, if any, and any other salaried musicians serving the church are directly or indirectly responsible to the music committee.

While many music committees serve out their terms without facing the necessity for the selection of a director of music, every committee is responsible for the quality of the director's work. If the committee considers his work unsatisfactory, some arrangement for improvement must be made. The director may respond to suggestions and criticism, or the committee may find it desirable to replace him. If, for any reason whatever, the committee is faced with the necessity of finding a new

47547

director, there are certain routine steps to take. First, the names of available directors must be obtained, by reference to music schools in the vicinity, by consultation with the local council of churches, by discreet advertisements in church papers or newspapers, by the pastor's questioning other ministers in the community.

After the names have been secured, the committee will go over the list and select the two or three whose qualifications seem best adapted to the position. If the director is at present employed, the committee may wish to go to his church and observe him in action. They may be able to decide on a man without having him conduct a service in the home church, although it will be well to confer with him at length as to the plans he could present and to give him a tryout on the organ if he is to be the organist.

In the event that the music committee is in a church where the director of music is not the organist, the committee may be obliged to engage an organist or pianist. The procedure will be much like that for a director, except that the director may have a man or woman to suggest. Ordinarily, an organist should not be engaged without the approval of the director. Too, an organist ought to be tried in a regular worship service before the engagement is made final.

Where there are paid soloists, the music committee may have to fill vacancies from time to time. Here, again, names of possible replacements can be obtained from the director or organist or both. The committee may wish to set apart an evening convenient to the committee members to hear soloists. All likely candidates may be invited to come for tryouts. They will be heard one by one, and privately. Even though the committee has the authority here, it is a part of wisdom to engage no one unacceptable to the director.

The committee will find the professional musicians easier to deal with than amateurs or volunteers. Inasmuch as many churches have a volunteer choir exclusively, the average music committee must know its responsibilities and duties in this field. Where there is a volunteer choir, the committee should see that the director is a person with ability to teach as well as to plan and conduct. It is a rare church that can muster enough able musicians from within its membership who do not require fundamental instruction. If a volunteer choir is thrown open to anyone who will come, the committee will find itself in a hopeless situation which will require years to rectify. The committee should insist that the director deal with an applicant for a choir position just as he would with a professional singer, that is to say, give him a private tryout. No matter who the applicant may be, he should be allowed to sing only if he is capable. If he has possibilities, he may be kept on a substitute list, with the understanding that he will attend all choir rehearsals.

In the long run, the music committee will find that the efficient way to deal with a volunteer choir is by hard and fast rules to be worked out with the director. For instance, the director may wish to set as a requirement that no one may sing on Sunday morning who has not appeared for the weekly rehearsal. This is a reasonable provision which the committee will do well to endorse. Other rules might be: no solos until the director considers the singer qualified, no changing of places in the choir loft, each member will sit where the director feels that the voice is needed; substitutes will be used only when the regulars are absent. If a choir is built around rules formulated by the music committee and agreed upon by the members, each new singer will understand the situation from the beginning. The committee should bear in mind that the music makes or mars a worship service.

Other duties of the music committee will include the obtaining of a reasonable appropriation for new music, the fostering of annual musical programs such as at Easter and Christmas, and the providing of a supper or party for the choir at least once a year.

The music committee should give a report at the annual meeting following its election.

The Ushers' Committee

The chairman of ushers is usually an elected officer. He is given the privilege of making up his own committee. In some churches the deacons act as the ushers in addition to their other duties. When this is the rule, it is often the custom for one deacon to be in charge of the ushering on one Sunday, with the freedom to select his helpers from among the members of the church, other deacons taking turns at this task throughout the year. Inasmuch as ushering is a big job in itself, a church usually finds that a special committee for this work is preferable to leaving it to the deacons. But, however the committee is formed, the tasks are the same.

If the chairman of ushers finds that he has enough help, including both older and younger men, to do the job adequately, he will first make up a chart of dates and responsibilities and give a copy of this chart to each usher. On the chart should be the request that an usher who is unable to keep his appointment notify the chairman as far in advance as possible.

The main task of the ushers is to greet and seat the congregation at the Sunday services and at other times when large meetings are held in the church. The chairman should not usher people personally, except in emergencies; his task is organization, oversight, and greeting. A full half hour before a service he should take his place in the lobby or narthex of the church and be prepared to greet the first arrival. He should not be burdened with the distribution of calendars or programs, for his is an extremely important task, to give a stranger his first impression of the church. The pastor may preach exceedingly well and yet be unable to bring back a visitor who has received a poor reception at the door. Cheerfulness without familiarity, courtesy without officiousness, friendliness without curiosity mark the good head usher. He will be careful not to extend his hand while a man is struggling with his coat. He should stand far enough within the lobby to permit the one entering to get his bearings before he is received. The head usher can do much to create and maintain the atmosphere of worship. His voice will be low, and he will see that persons are not seated during prayer, the reading of the Scripture, or at other times designated by the pastor.

The position of the assistant ushers will depend upon the architecture of the church. There should be one at each entrance from the lobby into the church. If there is but one main entrance, there should be two men stationed there awaiting the nod of the head usher. Within the church there should be someone at the head of each aisle. After greeting the persons entering, the head usher will pass them along to one of his assistants who in turn will direct them to an aisle usher. This will avoid a gathering of people at the back of the church, and it will

eliminate the wanderers who try to seek out places for themselves.

Except for the greeting by the head usher, ushering should
be done with little talking because within the church silence
should reign. An usher occasionally may need to ask, how
many? He need not ask preference of position but should
seat people so as to keep the congregation well forward and
well balanced in the church. The assistant ushers will help
in this by guiding the people to one side or the other until the
church is well filled. When the usher has reached the pew
selected, he should turn, place his hand on the pew in front of
the one selected, and smilingly bow his party into their places.

Two questions always arise in a discussion of ushering: First,
should everyone be shown to a seat? Strangers should receive this courtesy. A good committee of ushers will know
the favorite pews of regular members who sometimes welcome the courtesy of an usher who guides them to their pews.
The ushers will find that few members, and fewer strangers,
will object if ushering is made a real part of the church service. An usher should never ask if he may show a person to a
seat but do it as though it were the expected thing.

The second question is: When should calendars be handed
to the people? The head usher should be free to be the host
in the church, so the duty devolves upon the ushers inside
the sanctuary. The best time to present the calendar or bulletin
is as the people are seated. The usher should give the calendars
for the party to the last person seated.

Next in importance among the duties of ushers is the reception of the offering. Nothing varies so much in church services as the manner of taking the collection. Before the hour
of worship the head usher, or some other usher, ought to
check the offering plates to make sure that they are in their
proper place and that there are enough of them. In some
churches, the plates are at the front available for the pastor
to hand to the ushers; in other churches, the ushers bring them
forward when they come or pick them up from a table before
the pulpit. Custom varies as to the prayer, either before or
after the offering, and the return of the offering. If the prayer
comes before the offering, the ushers may not be required to
return the plates, but simply to hand them to the head usher
at the rear of the church. These details must be familiar to

the ushers. It is advisable to confer with a guest speaker during the absence of the regular pastor to come to an agreement as to the method to be employed.

Just before the time of the offering, the ushers will come quietly to the center aisle or to the aisle down which they are to march. The head usher will not take a plate, but he will remain at the rear to see that all is in order. While he is occupied with this detail and unable to greet people, an assistant usher should take his place in the lobby to welcome latecomers who may be asked to wait until the offering is over before they are seated.

Promptness in being assembled to march down the aisle at the moment the signal is given either by the pastor or the organist or a choral sentence is a great virtue for ushers. Marching two by two should be done as quietly as possible. If there is no music, the head usher will be within his rights to ask the pastor if this cannot be arranged. While the plates are being passed through the pews, there should be no greetings extended by the ushers. They should avoid, too, any shortcuts made by stretching across anyone in the pews. It is far better to go around to the other end of the pew even though there is but one person seated there. One method is to pass the plate halfway through the pew and have it returned to the same usher. The usher on the opposite aisle will cover the other half of the pew in the same way. Otherwise each usher starts the plate through a row, and the man at the other end receives it and returns it through an alternate row.

If the offering is to be returned to the front of the church, the head usher will see that his men are assembled and ready to march the moment the signal is given. After the plates are placed on the table, the ushers will march to the rear of the church together, not stopping off, one by one, at their family pews. Although it may be a sacrifice, it is generally preferable for the ushers to take seats at the rear of the church. Some important part of the service follows immediately after the offering, and the confusion of several men moving about the church to join their families is distracting. If the offering is left at the rear of the church, the head usher will be responsible for keeping it safe until he gives it over to the treasurer or other financial officer.

A third task of the ushers is that of registration. One

usher should be assigned to keep an accurate count of the people present at every service. The count for the day will be given to the pastor, clerk, or other official responsible for the records, and the head usher will incorporate it in his records. Strangers should be registered either in a visitors' book or by cards. If the cards are kept in the pews, a notice may appear in the calendar, or the aisle usher may request strangers to sign the visitors' cards and drop them on the offering plate. It is of great importance to secure the names and addresses of strangers.

There are other responsibilities to make an usher's life interesting. He should watch over the ventilation, closing and opening windows and drawing curtains when necessary, and he should check the thermostat in the heating season; he should know where the first aid kit is located and be quick to assist anyone who becomes faint or ill; he will keep an eye out for signals from the pastor and will give the pastor any essential information that may be needed before the service ends. A good time to do this is when the ushers go forward for the plates; a folded note can be slipped to the pastor unostentatiously.

The report of the head usher at the annual meeting will include attendance and registration information, a list of all regular and substitute ushers who have served during the year, and a word of gratitude to these men. If there is any other word for the ushers, it would be this: Try to dress conservatively and as uniformly as possible. Enter into the spirit of worship, and let ushering enhance the value of the service in small church or large.

The Pulpit Committee

There are two general philosophies concerning a pulpit committee. The first is that such a committee is needed only when the pulpit is vacant and a new pastor must be found. Churches following this procedure will elect such a committee at a special meeting and for the period of time necessary to choose the new minister. The other way of looking at the pulpit committee is from a wider angle of year-around service. Churches holding to this custom will elect a pulpit committee at the annual meeting each year, and the committee will hold office for one year. No church knows when there will be a pastoral change, and the theory is that the committee is ready to serve at any time and, of great importance, has informed itself as to the work of a good pulpit committee. In the event of an emergency much time is saved by having this group ready to function without delay. An annual committee such as this may have the further responsibility of arranging for supplies for the pulpit during the pastor's vacation, illness, or other unavoidable absence. In some instances such a committee is available for consultation with the pastor regarding changes in the platform arrangement or changes in the order of service. For additional material about pulpit supplies, look under the work of deacons in Chapter Three.

Now, the tremendous responsibility of finding a new pastor!

Whether an annual committee or a special committee, the pulpit committee, faced with the task of securing a new pastor, will follow the same routine, except that the annual committee will have informed itself as to the necessary steps, whereas the special committee must make this the first item on the agenda. It is assumed that the committee is organized, with chairman and secretary, and an accepted time and place of meeting.

Thinking of the prospect of the vacant pulpit, the committee will ask first, Who? Many names will come unsolicited. The news of a vacant pulpit will be spread by the members, the local press, the denominational papers, and the "grapevine." Immediately, especially if the pulpit is a desirable one, applications will come directly from ministers seeking a change and from friends of ministers recommending certain men. Although there is a strong feeling that a man ought not to apply personally, these self-applications ought not to be thrown out on that basis alone. There are exceptional cases where a man is not in a position to ask a secretary or other friend to speak for him. Some ministers have scruples about using their acquaintances for this purpose. The applications and recommendations should be sorted through with care. At least the names in this list are known to be *available*.

It is not likely, however, that a committee will wish to stop with this unsolicited list. On its own initiative, the committee will gather names. The state secretary of the denominational body, a city secretary, the dean of a seminary may be consulted confidentially. Men who have supplied the pulpit and who are remembered for their excellent work may be added to the list. The author of a book or of an article in a church paper may seem to have the necessary qualifications. Members of the church who travel widely, and new members who have come from other communities, may have some very helpful suggestions.

Once the list is large enough, the committee will go through it with care. Many of the names will be crossed off immediately for good reason, and the names of a few men who have the qualifications for the pulpit will be culled out. At this stage, the committee will need to secure the records of the men and to find out whether or not they are available. These are important steps. A man's record will tell more about him than his personal appearance or one excellent sermon. The committee will need to know how he stands up in a parish after he has been there for a while. It is not fair to assume that any man is available. A man may not have been at his present post long enough to make a change advisable; he may have no desire to change; he may be vital to the program where he is. Of course, such men might be tempted by a larger opportunity, better climate, better living conditions for the family, or by the challenge of an untried field. To tempt a man who is not actually available is most unwise on the part of a pulpit committee. Both the record and the availability of a man can be secured by the state or city denominational secretary without bringing the name of the church into the picture.

With the names of a few good men cleared, the committee is ready to make a selection. The time-honored way is for the committee, or representatives from it, to attend a service in the man's church without warning him. After all the men on the preferred list are heard, the committee is ready to decide on the man who is their choice for presentation to the church. This system has many faults, but it is far better than the custom followed by some churches of inviting a series of men to the church, and then holding a special meeting of the church to vote. Not only does this custom pit men against each other, but it upsets the unity of the church. Each one of the men will have pleased some, and the one receiving enough votes for a call will come to a church only to find that he has some people set against him from the beginning. Happily, ministers are rapidly putting an end to this unfortunate situation by refusing to present themselves as candidates in a series, and they insist that one be heard and acted upon before another is brought into the picture.

The ideal way would seem to be to make an appointment with a man who stands at the top of the list. By personal conference the committee can learn more than by listening to a chance sermon. A man's record will not lie, but one sermon might create an unfavorable impression which could well destroy the minister's chance. On the other hand, if, after a personal conference, the committee makes an appointment for the man to preach in the home church, the candidate will be able to prepare his sermon for the purpose. Another advantage of the conference plan is to check the man's availability and to outline to him the position which is vacant. Such details as salary, allowances, pension, vacation, parsonage, staff, the history of the church, the theological slant should be discussed frankly. Unless a man knows all of this, he might receive a call to the church only to turn it down after he is fully informed.

After the candidate is heard, the pulpit committee should arrange for a special meeting of the church just as soon as constitutionally possible. The church must be given the opportunity to act before the impressions of the Sunday have grown dim, and the candidate deserves to have a prompt decision. If the vote is favorable, the pulpit committee ought to telephone or telegraph the news to the candidate and make sure that a detailed, written call is sent to him by the clerk. The time of making the move and the matter of moving expenses ought to be clearly stated in the call.

A special committee will have no report except the presentation of the candidate, but an annual pulpit committee will give an account of itself at the annual meeting.

Other Committees

The four committees discussed are common to nearly all churches of congregational polity, but beyond these four there will be a wide divergence of custom. Some of the committees frequently found will be discussed in this section.

(*a*) The Baptismal Committee. A baptismal committee is often the deacons' wives or the deaconesses and deacons. The committee has the oversight of the baptismal robes and the preparation of the candidates for baptism. In Baptist churches, and in other churches practicing immersion, the men and women and children who are baptized often are dressed for the occasion in robes owned by the church. The committee will see that these robes are kept laundered, mended, and in every way presentable. New robes will be procured as needed. When the pastor announces the names of the candidates and the date of baptism, the committee will seek out the persons on the list and make arrangements to supply each with a robe of proper size. At the time of baptism, a deacon will be in the men's dressing room to assist if needed, and one or more of the women members will serve in the women's dressing room. A man and a woman will be stationed at the pool to receive the newly baptized persons and give them any assistance necessary as they return to the respective dressing rooms.

Baptism is a symbol of a spiritual experience. The committee should do everything possible to enhance its spiritual value. The committee is under the jurisdiction of the board of deacons and deaconesses.

(b) The Evangelism Committee. Its duties are to foster the evangelistic activities of the church over and above the regular program, the drawing up of a yearly plan of co-ordinated evangelistic effort in the church, the sponsoring of prayer groups dedicated to evangelistic projects, co-operation with denominational and interdenominational evangelistic "drives" or programs. This may be a subcommittee of the board of deacons or may be appointed by the church to work with them.

(c) The Missionary Committee. While the work of missionary education is definitely a part of Christian education, and is thus related directly to the board of Christian education in the local church, some churches feel it is essential to have a missionary committee which will help to determine and promote participation in the benevolence and missions budget in co-operation with the financial officers. In churches which feel that such a committee is desirable, care should be taken to integrate its work in every way with the missionary education program, and thus avoid overlapping of functions.

Committees having to do with the work of deacons, of trustees, board of Christian education, and the church school will be discussed in the chapters devoted to those subjects. For work of other committees, such as stewardship, confer with the Division of World Mission Support and other related agencies.

FOR STUDY AND DISCUSSION

1. Is a democratic election of church officers the prime requisite to a democratic church? If you think so, in the light of this importance, discuss the method of choosing officers in your church.
2. If you were on the music committee of your church, would you try to make any changes in the present program? Why?
3. Discuss the value of good ushering in the small church.
4. If you were a minister, how would you go about the problem of getting your name before a pulpit committee of a vacant church?
5. What committees should be added to the list in this text?

PROJECTS

1. Make a complete list of the committees in your church, together with the names of the chairmen. How are they appointed? Point out any obsolete committees which exist without active functions.
2. Interview the pastor and find out how he was called to this church, and whether or not he enjoyed the experience.

CLASS PROJECTS

Using Roberts *Rules of Order,* hold a formal meeting of some supposed committee. Discuss the value of formal procedure.

BIBLIOGRAPHY

Ban, Joseph D., *Manual for Preaching Missions and Visitation Evangelism.*

Calling a Baptist Pastor (leaflet).

Gilchrist, Jack, *The Vacant Pulpit.*

Johnson, A. D., *The Work of the Usher.*

Keech, William J., *Our Church Plans for Missionary and Stewardship Education.*

CHAPTER III

The Work of Deacons and Clerk

THE OFFICE of the one we term pastor, minister, or preacher, is referred to in the New Testament by words which are translated bishop, presbyter, or elder. There is no indication at all that there is a gradation in the pastoral office; the words are used synonymously so far as scholars are able to determine. When we find, then, that Paul, writing to Timothy in the words found in the third chapter of I Timothy, makes a distinction between bishop and deacon, we infer that two separate offices are being discussed. Inasmuch as we know that bishop means pastor, we suppose that deacon refers to a person engaged in the work given to the seven men chosen by the apostles to aid them in the distribution of alms and in visitation. In any event, deacon is the name long given to the man who does the work set forth in the sixth chapter of the Acts. This office, call it by whatever name you will, is the only one established in the early church with the exception of pastor. All other offices have a later origin. For this reason the deacon holds an important and essential office in his church.

I. The Board of Deacons

The Board of Deacons has a presiding officer—who may be elected by the deacons or who may come into the office by seniority, in which event he will be known as the Senior Deacon, often a secretary, and frequently a treasurer. Some boards prefer to have no secretary and treasurer in order to keep their transactions oral and off the record.

1. *Their number:* Because the account of the choosing of the first deacons gives seven as the number selected, some churches hold to the custom of electing seven deacons and no more. It is likely, however, that some division of districts, nationalities, or responsibilities called for seven men in that early situation. The number is not sacred and surely was not intended as a

precedent. For the most part, churches follow the principle laid down in Acts, chapter six, and elect the number of deacons necessary for the work to be done. Surely a church of two thousand members needs a larger board than a church of two hundred! The error is usually on the short side which loads too much work on each deacon. In a very small church there should be at least one deacon for every twenty-five members, but in larger churches provision should be made for at least one deacon for every fifty members; with a minimum of five for the small church and seven to twelve for a larger church. The constitution of the local church should designate the number of deacons, but should have some provision to increase the number in the event that the membership grows substantially.

2. *How chosen:* Deacons are elected by the church in its annual meeting, except that vacancies occurring by death or resignation may be filled by action at special meetings or in a manner authorized in the constitution. This office is one which cannot be filled hurriedly or haphazardly, and a church customarily gives more time and thought to the selection of deacons than to the choice of any other official except pastor.

3. *Term of office:* A pastor is called for an indefinite period, and other officials usually are elected for a year's term, but deacons present a peculiar problem. For many years Baptist churches held to the custom of electing deacons for a life term. This grew out of the custom of setting apart the men chosen, inasmuch as it was felt that an ordination could not be set aside at the next annual meeting: "once a deacon, always a deacon." Many of our churches elect their deacons for life as they have always done. Many other churches, however, set a definite limit to a deacon's term of office. In these churches, the popular period is three years, usually with the proviso that after three years a deacon must remain off the board for a year before he may be eligible for re-election. There are several reasons for this limited term: a candidate who appeared to have all the qualifications for the office may prove incapable or unworthy of the responsibilities attached; deaths and resignations are so few that the board often becomes static for five or more years at a stretch and tends to get into a rut; there is no room for new men and men with splendid possibilities for the task who have grown up in the church. A limited tenure permits the natural removal of the less fit, avoids hard feelings, and guaran-

tees the church the opportunity for utilizing the best of the younger and new men. Both systems, lifetime and limited term, have their advocates and, undoubtedly, there are good and bad features in each.

A church holding to the limited term for deacons usually has a by-law providing for rotation to avoid the election of a full board in any one year. By way of illustration: a church with a board of nine deacons will, at the first election, choose three men for a one-year term, three for a two-year term, and three for a three-year term. Thereafter, there will be three vacancies each year to which will be elected three deacons for the full three-year term. The annual change will equal one-third of the board. This system insures a preponderance of experienced men and a good proportion of men who come to the problems with a fresh viewpoint.

Churches using the lifetime plan will hold elections to fill vacancies only. Stability and the preservation of the established order, with more gradual changes in policy, mark this procedure.

4. *Qualifications:* For the qualifications of a deacon we turn to verses eight to thirteen in the third chapter of I Timothy. Perhaps nowhere is there to be found a better description of the ideal deacon. The insistence is upon character.

From this Scripture passage has emerged the church's picture of a deacon and his qualifications. He is to be a man of high morals, ideals, and practices; he is to be even-tempered in all things; he is, if married, to be an example in his home life; he is to be settled in his religious faith; he is to be a man whose life has been and continues to be an inspiration to his fellow churchmen.

Another qualification is that a man be willing and able to give time to his task. A saint who is so busy that he cannot do justice to the office is a poor prospect for the board. This is a place where the ornamental has little value, and where prestige is not necessary.

In some churches the constitution provides a minimum age for a deacon. For a long time the title, deacon, brought visions of an elderly man of sedate and pious and, often, severe mien. This concept is rapidly disappearing, especially in churches and communities where the limited term has been practiced for a generation, for at least one of the board is a young man, approximately twenty-five.

In churches having associate membership, there is often the added qualification, that the deacons must be from the regular membership, baptized by immersion.

A custom in many churches provides for some deaconesses as well as deacons. Their work is discussed in another section of this chapter.

5. *Installation:* The good habit of installing and consecrating new officials of a church is growing. Excellent services for such occasions may be found in some books of worship available from the various denominational publishing houses. In many churches, particularly in the ones using limited terms, the new deacons are included in the general service for all officials and are not singled out for special honor or emphasis. In other churches, particularly in the ones with lifetime deacons, an ordination service is held for the new deacons. Such a service will follow quite closely the pattern laid down for the ordination of a clergyman. The scriptural qualifications of a deacon will be read, stress will be placed on the sacredness of the office, the new deacons and the church will be charged with their respective responsibilities, and there will be a solemn closing service when the new deacons kneel and the hands of the ordained minister and deacons are placed upon their heads while prayers of consecration are offered.

6. *Duties:* The chief duty of a deacon is that laid upon Stephen and his six companions in the early church, namely to assist the pastor and relieve him of the less exacting of his many tasks. In that early day this assistance took the form of distributing alms and visiting the sick, almost exclusively. Today, the deacon's duty is far more complex. It is the custom in some churches for the board to draw up a schedule at the beginning of the year, assigning men to the various types of responsibility that may arise during the church year.

(*a*) *Assistance with the ordinances.* Here is where all too many deacons and churches stop. Assistance with the ordinances is the public part of the deacon's work, and often the most coveted. It is, however, but a small part of the total job.

(1) The Ordinance of the Lord's Supper. When Communion is to be served, the preparation is in the care of the deacons. The communion table and the deacons' chairs will be arranged either the night before

the service or prior to the time the worshipers gather. Hymnals, offering plates, and other equipment should be arranged beforehand.

Fresh bread will need to be cut in small squares in sufficient quantity to care for the number of communicants. If the bread trays are to be covered, the doilies should be laundered for each usage. The pastor may prefer to have one or more pieces of bread left uncut to be broken by him during the ritual; in this event such pieces will be placed on the plate nearest the pastor's chair. Near him, too, will be a finger bowl of fresh water covered with a folded napkin for his use before breaking the bread.

The grape juice must be fresh. The cups or glasses must be immaculate and be free of dust or lint. When the deacons have prepared the bread and juice, they will arrange the plates and trays on the table and cover them with an immaculately clean cloth. Following the service, all plates and cups should be washed and stored carefully.

Before the service, the deacons should hold a brief rehearsal in order that each man may be sure of his position and part in the ceremony. It will be wise for the men to plan beforehand what they will wear. Dark suits and ties are preferable and should be neatly pressed.

If the pastor is in the habit of serving home communion to the sick and shut-ins, he will need one or more deacons to help him. They should take the responsibility for filling the small communion kit with the necessary elements. Communion to chronic invalids may be served in homes after regular communion services as an extension of the service held in the church, or it may be served at other times.

(2) The Ordinance of Baptism. The deacons, assisted by the deaconesses, are responsible for oversight of the committee on baptism. Their work is described in chapter two.

(*b*) *Sponsoring candidates for membership*. Usually persons desiring to unite with the church will make their request to the pastor, and he will arrange a conference with the deacons.

Persons who apply for admission to church membership following baptism are instructed by the pastor, usually in membership preparatory classes. After the pastor is satisfied that the candidates are ready for baptism and church membership, he will bring them before the deacons for questioning and approval or rejection. If the pastor feels that a candidate lacks the necessary Christian experience, he may prefer to have the advice of the deacons before postponing the baptism. Questions of the deacons to the candidate on such occasions are of a nature to test the sincerity of purpose and the extent of the Christian experience. The growth of the new Christian should be an important consideration in his conference with pastor and deacons.

Others may desire to unite with the church "on experience," having lost their relationship with the home church by extended absence, by the closing of the church, or for some other reason. After talking with them, the pastor will present them to the deacons. The questions often will be much the same as those put to unbaptized candidates. The point will be to determine whether or not prospective members have been awakened to their need for a church home to the point where they will not be tempted to drift away again.

The third class of candidates will be people who bring letters from other churches, indicating that they are in "good and regular standing." There is little to be discussed in such instances except that it is well for the deacons to become acquainted with them. The deacons may wish to question them about their activities in the former church in order that such information may be helpful in building the new members into the life of the church.

When the church comes together to vote on the acceptance of new members, the deacons will report their findings and advise the reception of the candidates. The advice of the board of deacons will mean much to a church in this instance, inasmuch as the majority of the members will not have met the newcomers. They can, therefore, vote intelligently only after having had the facts presented by the deacons.

(c) *Visitation or watchcare.* Beyond and above the more public duties of the deacons, in time involved and probably in importance, is the matter of the oversight of a number of members. After the board of deacons is made up for the year, the chairman or senior deacon will secure a list of the membership, with addresses, from the clerk or church secretary. The chairman will call a meeting of the board and the pastor, at which time the membership list will be distributed among the active deacons. If there are three hundred members, for example, and six deacons, each man will receive approximately fifty as his responsibility. If the community is large, a geographical distribution is wise, but in a small community matters of family ties, business alliances, and other relationships are important. The aim will be to give each deacon the persons whom he can serve to the best advantage. It is often wise to change the lists each year so that, barring exceptional cases, the deacons will have some new people every twelve months. In this way a deacon will become intimately acquainted with a large number of the membership during his term of office. After the lists are established, three copies of each should be typed, an original and two carbons, one for the deacon whose list it is, one for the chairman, and one for the pastor. In the event of misfortune or need in a parish home, there will be no doubt as to which deacon should be notified. After the deacon receives his list of the members under his care, he will begin the year's work.

First, he may like to write a letter to go to every home on his list. If he considers himself a poor letter writer, he can receive confidential help from the pastor. Personal letters are best, but if the work involved is too great, the following mimeographed letter (with deacon's signature) will serve:

Dear (name to be inserted) :

At a recent meeting of our Board of Deacons, of which I am a member, we were discussing the privileges and obligations of having been elected to this office. We were concerned particularly about the opportunities for being of inspiration and help to the other members of the church. The names of the members were divided so that each Deacon has a group which he can think of, in a sense, as his family for the next few months.

I am happy to say that your name is included among the others given to me, and I should like to call at your home soon to get better acquainted and to discuss the work which we do together in the church.

In the meantime, and at all times, I hope that you will feel free to get in touch with me if something occurs in your church relationship, or in your family or personal life, with which I, or someone else, might be able to be of assistance.

You have my very best wishes for a successful year in every way and especially in the life of the Spirit.

Sincerely,

About a week after sending out his letter, the deacon will begin calling in the homes. He will plan to visit in every home on his list within the year. The calls are best made when there is an opportunity to find the entire family at home, usually early in the evening. These calls will disclose facts which the pastor should know. There may be illness, unemployment, change of residence, a new baby, a disgruntled attitude toward the church. The deacon can do much to aid his church by interpreting the church program and the pastor's work. The deacon will find circumstances in some homes which make it wise to call several times during the year. This will be true of the sick and shut-ins.

As the deacon gets to know his people by sight, if he does not know them already, he should check the congregation on Sunday to note the absentees on his list. After a person is absent for three consecutive Sundays, he should call at the home, if it has not been possible before. Another way of making this check is to take a registration on Communion Sunday. Cards printed for this purpose are available and they may be placed in the pew racks. The pastor may request that everyone present register. Following the service, the deacons may take the cards and sort them out, giving each man his own people.

New members, as they are added to the church, will be placed on the deacons' lists. These additions deserve immediate and active follow-up until they are well assimilated into the life of the church.

(d) *Pulpit supplies.* The task of supplying the pulpit during the pastor's absence falls to the deacons' lot unless it is assigned to a pulpit committee. Such absences will occur during illness, vacation, and when the pastor is invited to speak elsewhere. Occasionally, the pastor may exchange with another pastor for a Sunday or for a vacation period. It is customary for the pastor to confer with the deacons before accepting such invitations. The deacons also may be called upon to select or pass upon special speakers at times when the pastor is not absent. Usually the pastor will supply the name or names of his choice of substitute for his pulpit, but it is the prerogative of the deacons to approve or reject. If the matter of finding substitute preachers is left entirely to the deacons, they will have available the names of former supplies and former pastors who should be invited for special celebrations of historic significance. Speakers may be sought through the state convention office also.

The deacons must arrange for the payment of the honorarium; the check should be secured from the treasurer in advance, so that the man may be paid while he is there. Many preachers operate on a small budget, and if they advance expense money from their own pockets it may create hardship if it is not refunded promptly. When the man is invited to speak, the amount of the honorarium should be named, and directions given as to transportation and how to find the church. In some instances, a deacon will be delegated to meet the speaker at the station. Always, one or more deacons will be present at the church to greet the man and show him to the study, explain the order of service, and give other assistance. Some churches prefer that a deacon sit on the platform and introduce the guest. If the speaker is obliged to stay in the community for a meal or night's lodging, the deacons should take care of this. If a hotel reservation is to be made, the deacons will do this in advance.

(e) *Custodians of the Fellowship Fund.* A survey has shown that the majority of Baptist churches have a Fellowship Fund made up of communion offerings. The board of deacons has charge of this money and its distribution. The use of it is confidential and ought to be known only by the deacons and pastor. This fund is a sacred trust and is not available for any purpose other than the relief of needy within the parish unless otherwise designated, as for instance the annual offering for the Ministers and Missionaries Benefit Board. If the deacons see an urgent outside need which seems to them worthy, or if they have pressure put upon them by other church officials, they are morally obliged to present the issue to the church in a regular or special meeting before dipping into the fund. When there is need in the home of a member or other person who is definitely the responsibility of the church, the deacons should meet with the pastor and discuss the problem of alleviating the financial crisis. In some instances money will be the wisest gift, in many others food, fuel, or clothing. In extraordinary cases the deacons will find it wise to discharge a debt by dealing directly with the creditor rather than with the family. There will be times when a proffered loan will be much better than an outright grant. After the board has decided on the ways and means and the amount, one or more deacons or the pastor will be delegated to take the gift to the home. Where the need promises to be of long standing, the deacons will decide the amount of weekly or monthly help during the crisis. The account of receipts and expenditures very rarely includes names. An expenditure will be recorded simply: "April 12, rent $24," "June 4, gift $10." A code may be used, having name and number in a confidential file and only the number in the account book. This avoids making a record of the names of the beneficiaries and often saves the feelings of good and useful members of the church.

(f) *Board of Review.* The board of deacons is called upon occasionally to serve as a board of review to pass upon the seemliness and advisability of suggested new activities to be held in the church building. For instance, one municipality requested the use of the basement rooms of the church as a polling place during election. The pastor rightly conferred with the deacons about this matter. Any group, men or women or young people, who want to put on money-making projects or activities that might be questioned as to propriety, in the church or in the name of the church, should confer with the deacons before initiating the activity. This counseling function of the deacons is a delicate one, but quite essential. If any organizations or group of members were permitted to use the building without due consideration for the good of the whole body, the church's reputation and usefulness might be impaired. It is unwise to place this responsibility on the pastor alone. If a pastor permits or forbids an activity, he brings down wrath upon his head, but if the board of deacons makes the same decision, there is the feeling that a democratic process has been followed.

(g) *Pastor's acolytes.* The word "acolyte" is not often used in a Baptist church, but it well expresses what is meant here. The deacons are in no real ecclesiastical order, but they are in an office which is honored by other laymen. The church platform and the pulpit come under the jurisdiction of the deacons. The board should assign men who, early Sunday morning, should check to see that the platform or chancel is neat and orderly, that the pastor's Bible and hymnbook are on the stand. If the preacher likes a glass of water available, the deacons in charge should put a glass with fresh, cool water in a place arranged for it. Unless it is against the pastor's wishes, the deacons should visit him in the study before the service to inquire if there are other needs to be met. If the minister wears a robe, a deacon might help him put it on.

(h) *Responsibility for spiritual phases of the work.* Some churches delegate the promotion of evangelistic efforts to a committee on evangelism, but others assume that the board of deacons is the proper body to care for all special evangelistic emphases. In the latter type of church the deacons will give attention to a year's program of evangelism under the direction of the pastor.

In any church there are other phases of evangelism which the board will manage, and in all churches the deacons will be the prime movers to keep a high spiritual atmosphere in all departments of the work. If their church maintains a midweek service or prayer service, they will be expected to attend and assist to the limit of their time and ability. The pastor will be better prepared for the pulpit if one or more deacons meet with him before services for prayer. If the choir gathers in a separate room, other deacons will meet there for a prayer. The office of deacon is primarily a spiritual office, and the spiritual level of a church will depend to a large extent upon the life and conduct and church activity of the men on the board.

II. Deaconesses

In many Baptist churches the board of deacons is supplemented by a group of deaconesses. The deaconesses are chosen in much the same way as the deacons and for the same reasons.

The deaconesses rarely have the privilege of serving communion, but they may prepare the elements and take charge of the plates, trays, and cloths, and wash the cups. They have specific responsibility in baptismal services, especially for women and children. Visitation, especially in homes where the call of a deacon might prove embarrassing or unwelcome, is the chief task of the deaconesses. Usually these women have more time during the day for such tasks than do the deacons, so much of the relief work in the parish and hospital calls fall to their lot. Often they have their own organization and meet with the deacons only at stated times. Some churches, however, place the two groups on a par, and they are in one organization with equal voting privileges.

III. Junior Deacons

A growing movement among the churches is the maintenance of a body of junior deacons. Boys, and sometimes girls, of teen-age are elected at the annual meeting for the purpose of training for later responsibility. The junior deacons are in much the same category as the young people who take over the city government once a year in the "Junior Citizens" project. The organization of junior deacons is for training and encouragement only. They will be asked to usher occasionally; may be on the platform to read the scripture and help with other parts of the worship service; they may be invited to sit in on a meeting of the board of deacons; and they may be given the responsibility of calling at the homes of people their own age. In some churches the Junior Board of Deacons is composed of people between the ages of twenty and thirty-five, in which event this Board shares the same responsibility as the Senior Board of Deacons. Usually this arrangement is found only in large churches and is for the purpose of preparing younger men, or in the case of deaconesses, younger women, for the heavy responsibilities of the diaconate.

IV. The Clerk

The clerk is elected at the annual meeting of the church, and for a one-year term. His, however, is one office having no bar to re-election. Inasmuch as the qualifications for clerk are peculiar, and the time required to do the work rather long, a good clerk often retains his office for a decade or longer. After the pastor, he is the man who knows most about the membership, statistics, and trends of the church life.

In order to be effective, the clerk must write a legible hand, have some knowledge of simple bookkeeping procedure, be by nature accurate and prompt, and have infinite patience. To this must be added a character which will command the respect of the membership and the community, for the clerk is often the representative of the church in matters of public relations. Many churches elect a woman to this office rather than a man.

Duties of the Clerk

1. *Keeping the minutes.* The clerk must be present, or have a substitute present, at all regular and special meetings of the church. In some instances he will be asked to serve as secretary of special committees or boards whose minutes should become part of the church record. He will make an accurate record of the proceedings of these church meetings and later inscribe the

permanent record in a book which the church will provide. The importance of the accuracy and legibility of the minutes cannot be overestimated inasmuch as later generations, and sometimes courts, will have no other means of knowing the transactions of the church. The clerk is, in a real sense, an historian, compiling the history of his church month by month and year by year. Not only future generations but the present generation will depend upon him, because his reading of the "minutes of the last meeting" will bring to light unfinished business and other items which might slip by except for his carefully made record.

2. *Implementing the minutes.* As a church meeting proceeds, there will be committees appointed. Some of the appointees will be present, others may not. However, even though all the appointees are on hand to hear of their new responsibility, the clerk notifies every person elected or appointed at the meeting. His letter will contain an excerpt from the minutes that will advise the member of his appointment and also of the duties imposed upon him. In church meetings he may be authorized to write letters of thanks, condolence, expostulation. Promptly, following the meeting, the clerk will write these letters, retaining a copy which will become a part of the minutes. It may be stated here that the clerk is to attach to the minutes copies of all letters which he writes for the church. In addition to appointments and letters, a church meeting may direct a functioning committee or board to take some action on an issue brought before the church. The clerk will write to the chairman of that committee or board, quoting the minutes pertinent to the situation. An efficient chairman will refuse to do the thing suggested until he has the official word in writing from the clerk. The clerk should send to the pastor and the moderator of the church copies of the minutes. Usually, there are items of unfinished business that require some thought or preparation on the part of the moderator before he can present them intelligently at the next regular or special meeting.

3. *Keeping the church roll.* If any task of the clerk is more important than all others it is keeping the church roll. The members are the church, and only by an accurate record of the names and addresses of the members can a church be kept an efficiently functioning unit. Even in small communities,

or in small churches in large communities, the turnover of the membership is surprisingly high. The pastor and clerk can help each other by reporting all changes that come to their attention. The church roll is the basis of all church mailings of letters and literature; it is the field of operation for the Every Member Canvass committee; it is necessary to the deacons for the formulation of their responsibility lists; it is the Mecca for persons in the church who need to know sex and age groupings; associational dues are levied on the reported membership; and denominational statistical reports rely upon it. A membership roll to which have been added all new members to date, from which have been removed the deceased and transferred, that shows the changes in names due to marriage and the changes in address due to moving is an invaluable asset to any church. The responsibility for this roll is the clerk's.

By a code indication, or by means of separate lists—the latter is preferable—the clerk will keep his roll in such a way as to indicate resident and nonresident members, regular members, and associate members in churches having this dual relationship, and, if such a division has been established by the church, the active and inactive members. Some churches have constituent members, people who attend and contribute but who do not join the church. All divisions of membership recognized in the church must be marked clearly on the roll.

In addition to the book containing the roll of current members, the clerk will need to keep a card index including a card for every person who is or ever has been a member of the church. He may use guide cards to separate the various classifications, but in his own way he will keep a card for everyone. This card should be as complete as possible. It should show the date of accession—when the name was first added to the roll; the date of baptism, if the member was baptized in that church; the address; and the age if possible. When a member dies or takes his letter to another church the data should be entered on the card. This record is valuable not only to the church but often in courts of law for the issuing of certificates of birth, the granting of passports, or the settling of estates. Families may need to refer to it to settle uncertainties of property claims or ancestry.

4. *Custodian of the records*. In addition to his own book of minutes and files, the clerk will be in charge of the records

of past years, of deeds and titles, of such minutes of church organizations as seem worthy of a place in the church history, of the church charter, and of the seal of the church. He will see to it that the most valuable and rarely used records and other important items are kept in a safe or bank deposit box. In many states, the Department of Archives will receive for safe-keeping the old records of a church, returning a photostatic copy to the clerk for church reference. The denominational historical society will do the same.

5. *Announcements and publicity.* The charter or constitution of most churches provides for a legal notice of church meetings to be placed in a newspaper or to be mailed to the members a specified number of days before the meeting. This is another job for the clerk. If he fails in this, it can mean that the meeting must be postponed. In cities, reporters will often phone the clerk after a meeting to secure newsworthy items. If he is not called, the clerk owes it to the church to mail to the local newspaper a résumé of the more important items of business.

6. *Preparation of reports.* Growing in popularity is the custom of assembling the reports of the various church activities to be put in a booklet for distribution to the members present at the annual meeting. Where this system is used, the clerk, unless a separate committee has been appointed, will be the collector and editor of material. In any event, he must prepare an annual report of his own for the church showing the accessions, removals, and present total membership. He is the one who supplies the association or state obituary committee with the names of the members of his church who have died during the church year. He will be required to fill out the report for the association minutes. Whenever any agency of government or a church requests a report, the letter will be referred to the clerk.

7. *Dismissal of members.* Forms for the dismissal of members by letter will be kept in stock by the clerk. The denominational publishing house can provide these, or the church may have a printed form of its own. Whenever a member requests the transfer by letter to some other church, and the request is granted in church meeting, the clerk will fill out one of these forms and mail it to the clerk of the church to which the member is going. Usually there is a stub on the form which is to be

returned to the clerk after the member is received. If this is not received in due time, the clerk should write for an explanation. Theoretically, the member remains on the one church roll until notice of reception in another church has been filed. Likewise, members coming by letter from other churches will bring or have forms sent from those churches. Until the clerk has these in his possession, the church cannot receive the new members.

FOR STUDY AND DISCUSSION

1. Using a concordance, refer to the passages in the New Testament where the word "deacon" appears. On the basis of this reference, discuss the appropriateness of the title as applied to the work of deacons in your church.

2. Discuss the qualifications for the office of deacon listed in the text, subtract from them any which seem non-essential, and add others which may seem needful to you in your situation.

3. Talk over the advantages and disadvantages of having (*a*) deaconesses; (*b*) junior deacons.

4. Compare the office of deacon with the offices of other workers in the church at the point of spiritual opportunity and community prestige for the church.

5. With the pages devoted to the work of the clerk before you, make up a list of the desirable qualifications for a "good" clerk.

PROJECTS FOR CLASS REPORT

1. By conferring with the clerk, secure the present number of active members of the church. Then set down the number of active deacons. Ascertain the number of people who would be the responsibility of one deacon. Recommend improvement in the present setup if it be necessary.

2. Write down the deacons' duties. Interview three deacons, and have them check those duties which they consider essential. Approach two other people with the same request, and then the pastor. Analyze the answers for the class.

3. Watch a communion service in your church or some other,

and write an account of the part played by the deacons.

4. Ask the clerk for a copy of the minutes for the last regular meeting. Go through the minutes and point out to the class how many notifications and letters the clerk was required to write after this one meeting. List the items of unfinished business which must be brought up at the next meeting.

CLASS PROJECT

Using available church forms, work out suggestions for improving forms for a church, including the letter of dismissal of a member and a card for the membership roll. Ask the pastor or clerk to attend a later session of the class and comment on the forms contrived.

BIBLIOGRAPHY

Grenell, Z. and Goss, A., *The Work of the Clerk.*
Thomas, Donald F., *The Deacon in a Changing Church.*
Torbet, Robert G., *A History of the Baptists.*

CHAPTER IV

The Work of Financial Officers

THE HUMBLEST BIT of work done for a church has a definite spiritual content; therefore it is incorrect to divide church tasks between the spiritual and material. In other words, it is straying from the real fact to state bluntly that the deacons are "spiritual" officers and the trustees "material" officers. Nevertheless, a local church does have assets which are material before the law. These are the real estate and church building, often a parsonage, movable equipment of various kinds, funds invested in stocks and bonds, and cash on hand. The deacons have enough to do so there must be officers to take the burden of safeguarding the tangibles of the church. This chapter will deal with the business officers of a church.

I. The Board of Trustees

The common term for the group of people elected to care for the property of a church is the Board of Trustees or Stewards. In some states, the title of trustee is designated in the charter, and the churches in those states have little or no choice in the matter. The title is of little consequence, except that steward is expressive and explanatory of the function of this board. As stewards they hold in trust for the church membership the material possessions accruing to the church. An autonomous church, such as a Baptist church, holds title to all property which is donated to it or purchased by it. Of course, the church has the inalienable right to vote on the disposition of the assets, but, to comply with the law and to be assured of skilled administration of assets, it is necessary to empower representatives to hold property, to administer it, and to handle all legal and financial details relating to the property. The trustees have these responsibilities and others that the church may assign to them. For ordinary administration the members of the board are competent, by granted powers, to act on their own initiative; on all unusual matters the church members vote.

1. *The number of trustees.* The number of trustees is often smaller than the number of the deacons. The deacons must deal with people, but the trustees deal with property and with figures. Even in a very large church the board need not be large, except for the advantage of the advice of the largest number of able men available. Most frequently found is a board composed of from five to seven men.

2. *How elected.* The trustees are customarily elected by the church in annual meeting, in classes, as are the deacons. In some churches the trustees are eligible for re-election without the lapse of a year, but increasingly the custom is to provide for a year off, as is true of the Deacons and other major boards of a church.

3. *Qualifications.* The character and devotion of a trustee should equal that of a deacon, for he is to handle the dedicated offerings of followers of Christ. The public, however, does not always require so much of him in careful living as it does of a deacon. The difference in duties explains this attitude. A trustee needs not only excellent character, with stress on scrupulous honesty, but he needs practicality, thriftiness, financial ability, and good judgment. A working knowledge of law is a great asset. A gem of a trustee is a man who has all the other attributes and is successfully conducting a business of his own. Qualified women provide a new source for board membership.

4. *Duties.* The trustees hold the property of the church. Signatures of certain officers in the board are required on all deeds, transfers of stock, bank notes, and mortgages, upon authorization of the church. Ordinarily the personal property of the trustees is not assessable or involved, even upon the failure of the church to make good on a financial obligation if the instrument has been properly drawn. The trustees will need to have legal advice whenever a note, mortgage or other obligation is contracted, to make sure that they are not personally liable. The titles to property, stocks and bonds, cash, and other church assets are in their keeping. They receive and disburse negotiable assets for the church. If the church is heir to a legacy, the proceedings for receiving it are in the hands of the trustees; they will listen to the reading of the will and protect the rights of the church. When the estate is settled, the proceeds will be added to other assets being held for the church.

The same holds true of current gifts and contributions.

The disbursement of funds according to the will of the church will be cared for by the trustees. They will give an account to the church annually, or oftener, of the property in their keeping. A detailed report of receipts and expenditures, dormant funds, and pieces of real estate will be submitted to the church as required. The ability to make such reports requires the keeping of books and other records.

The trustees will endeavor to maintain or improve the property which has been given into their care. If there are trust funds consisting of stocks and bonds, they will keep a careful watch of the record of the companies in which the money is invested and will advise the church when it seems wise to sell the holding and reinvest it. They will arrange for all minor repairs to the building or buildings and advise the church when a major repair or improvement seems essential to preserve the value of the real estate.

5. *The composition of the board.* Some churches elect trustees and grant to them the privilege of deciding in their own meeting the responsibility which each man is to carry. Other churches elect trustees and also elect a treasurer of the church, a financial secretary, and one or more assistants as the situation may require. A finance committee and a budget committee may be elected by the church. Sometimes a separate Every Member Canvass committee also is elected. In any event, all of these financial officers are related to the board of trustees, either as regular members or as ex officio members. Their responsibilities intermesh to such an extent that no one of them can work independently of the others. Since the Canvass committee has others besides financial leaders in its membership, it may act also in a consultative relationship.

II. Other Financial Officers

1. *The Treasurer.* The treasurer of a church holds one of the most important posts. He receives but rarely the amount of gratitude due him for the time and thought he puts into his work. This attitude on the part of his fellow members is due to the fact that the treasurer frequently must point out the need for the payment of back pledges, and he must hesitate to appropriate money for popular causes when the assets show that

the expenditure is unwise. The treasurer has several well-defined duties.

(a) *Custodian of liquid assets.* While the board of trustees has the oversight of the long-range financing of the church, the treasurer devotes much of his time to the immediate financing. The offerings placed on the plates at the Sunday services and the checks which come through the mail go to the treasurer for deposit. He knows the balance on hand and can, by referring to the budget, determine whether or not the funds are coming in at the proper rate.

(b) *Paymaster.* All bills which the church incurs go to the treasurer for payment. In the budget are fixed items, such as salaries, fuel, upkeep. The treasurer will check each bill to make sure that it covers an expense authorized in the budget adopted by the church. The salaries, telephone, gas, electricity, and other regular expenses he will pay on his own initiative, but all other bills, even though they are in accord with the budget, he will have O.K.'d by the person who made the purchase or contracted for the service. This is a wise and customary precaution. If he detects a bill which is not included in a budgetary item, which exceeds the allotment in the budget, or which has not been authorized in a church meeting, he should refuse to pay it until he asks for instructions from the board of trustees or the church. In small churches, the treasurer will be able to regulate the expenses and have a full knowledge of the church obligations, but in a large church there will be a great number of people with power to charge things to the church account, and this will complicate his task. To a great extent, the credit standing of a church in its community is dependent upon the treasurer. The promptness with which he pays the bills and the ruggedness with which he holds the church within its financial abilities will determine the standing of the church. This has a spiritual value: a defaulting, almost bankrupt church cannot impress its community favorably.

(c) *Banker.* Even in the smallest communities, a church treasurer will have banking facilities available near-by. Payment by check is the custom and cash payments are rare. In the event that a cash payment is made, the treasurer must insist upon a receipted bill. Even though the church may have every confidence in his integrity, he should have, for his own protection and satisfaction, some sort of voucher for every cent paid out. The canceled check is an automatic voucher, as is a receipted bill. The church check book is the exclusive responsibility of the treasurer. If the church authorizes a loan from the bank on recommendation of the trustees, it is usually the treasurer's responsibility to arrange it, and it is his task to make the repayment when due. If the current expense balance is large enough at certain times of the year to warrant placing a part of it in a savings account, he will see to this.

(d) *Bookkeeper.* The treasurer must keep, or cause to be kept, accurate records of the receipts and expenditures. In addition to the current funds, he will have a book to record the condition of trust funds, special funds, and real estate. He must be able to give the church a monthly, quarterly, or annual report of the finances, and he must be able to keep the trustees posted on the condition of all of the church assets.

2. *Assistant Treasurer.* Only large churches find it necessary to have one or more assistant treasurers. In a small church, the offerings to be counted and wrapped will not be so great that the treasurer will find himself swamped. A treasurer in the smallest church, however, is wise to have some other official, a deacon perhaps, with him at the time he counts the money. This is to prevent any possible error. In churches having at least one assistant treasurer this problem is solved. Also when the treasurer is out of town on vacation or business or laid aside by illness, the assistant may be given power of attorney or be so authorized by the church that he may do the treasurer's most pressing work in the interim. The post of assistant treasurer is a good training field, and the church may be preparing against the day when a new treasurer is needed.

3. *The Financial Secretary.* In smaller churches, this post often is held by the treasurer, and the one man handles both jobs capably. A medium-sized or large church finds the need for a man to be financial secretary and nothing else. The chief tasks of the secretary are to keep a record of the pledges made by the members and to count the loose offering. After the pledges are received at the beginning of the church year, the financial secretary will prepare a book or card-file showing the name and amount of the pledge. The record will be in alphabetical order. On Sunday, after either the treasurer or the financial secretary has removed the money from the envelopes

and checked the amount on the envelopes, the other officer will be given the empty envelopes and he will credit against the pledges the sums marked.

In many churches the financial secretary takes charge of the offering and checks the money in the envelopes. After he has finished, he either gives the bag of cash to the treasurer with a slip showing his calculation of the amount, or he actually makes the bank deposit and turns the deposit slip over to the treasurer. There are several advantages in having the secretary handle the offering. Many people will not mark the amount on the front of the envelope, many will put the entire sum in one side of a duplex envelope, and some will put a double amount in one envelope, having destroyed the one for the week previous. With his pledge book before him, the secretary is able to figure out just how the money is to be credited. Also, it is easier to keep separate the amount received on pledges and the amount of loose offerings. Many treasurers and financial secretaries prefer to work together, thus preventing any possible oversight or error.

This work of the treasurer and financial secretary is confidential.

In many churches the secretary is required to prepare and send out statements either quarterly or semi-annually to the members, showing the condition of their pledges. It is wise to send out a statement to everyone, even to those whose pledges are up to date. This custom avoids creating the impression that the delinquents are being dunned. A member who is unaccustomed to receiving statements may resent it at first, but soon he is likely to favor the system as it keeps him informed as to the credit given him and gives him the opportunity to correct any errors which may have occurred.

A financial secretary may exert a quiet, spiritual influence among the membership. If he observes that a man is making the same pledge year after year, although his financial condition is steadily improving, he may be able to point out to him the principle of giving "as he has been prospered." Oftentimes, a church member would make a larger pledge if he realized that his was out of proportion to the giving of others of the same income. There is nothing which promotes spiritual growth more than a deep sense of stewardship obligation toward the material things of life. Jesus pointed this out by telling his followers that "where a man's treasure is, there will his heart be also." The financial secretary is in a unique position to guide his fellow members tactfully into more adequate giving.

The report of the financial secretary will not be detailed. At the end of the year he will list the total amount pledged, the total amount paid against pledges, and the balance either way. Sometimes the church will ask that he tabulate the pledges to show how many members pledge and how many pledges are ten cents a week, fifty cents, and so on. He will show the current expense and benevolences in separate columns.

4. *Assistant Financial Secretary.* In churches where the burden of work on the financial secretary is great, he may be provided with one or more assistants. This post is a good place to train a future secretary.

5. *Treasurers and Secretaries of Benevolence.* Churches that use duplex envelopes usually have a separate staff of treasurers and secretaries to handle the benevolence funds. All money given in the benevolence side of the duplex envelopes, and all donations designated for missions or charity will be turned over to the benevolence treasurer for recording and disbursing. The duties of these officers parallel those of the current expense officers. Sometimes the treasurer of the church serves as treasurer of both funds and keeps the money either in two accounts or in a joint account. In this instance, the secretary of benevolences will keep an account of the money received by means of a voucher given to him by the treasurer after the offerings have been counted and tabulated, and he will disburse money by drawing an order on the treasurer. In some churches the financial secretary keeps the pledge book for both current expense and benevolences, and the church elects a treasurer for each fund. The local situation will determine how many officers are needed.

6. *The Finance Committee.* The finance committee is often a committee of the board of trustees, a group of men and women responsible for planning to finance the church's activities. Unless the church elects separate committees for the budget and Every Member Canvass, the finance committee will assume these responsibilities. If there are separate committees, the finance committee will be found, usually, to be made up of that part of the board of trustees charged with the money and investment matters, while other members of the board look to the upkeep of the real estate.

7. The Budget Committee. The duties of this committee will not vary with the manner of election, but forward-looking churches have come to realize that it is not wise to expect the trustees, finance committee, or other regular officers of the church to take on the responsibility of preparing an annual budget. For one reason, these men, by the nature of their work, find it necessary to keep down expenses as much as possible, and to compare the current year with previous years in reference to costs, upkeep, etc. If a church appoints a special budget committee of people who are concerned more with the program and outreach of the church, they will be able to exercise uninhibited vision and faith, and draw up a proposed budget which, although it is almost sure to need revision after the Every Member Canvass, will serve to raise the sights of the people and to point out to them many of the aspects of the church's mission which could be realized by going forward in confidence and sacrifice. The following paragraphs are written from a common-sense viewpoint, but into them should be read the possibility for the budget committee, at its first suggestion, to be less restrained than a traditional viewpoint has warranted.

The committee will need to recognize, first, whether or not the budget to be drawn up is to be inclusive. The old type budget was one which provided for church expenses only and did not take into account the various organizations of the church; the inclusive type budget provides for all organizations such as the church school, youth fellowship, woman's society. The committee must determine what kind of budget the church has authorized them to prepare. If the organizations are to be included, the officers of those organizations will be asked for itemized statements showing their financial needs for the next year and their probable income.

To arrive at the figures for the budget, the committee will discuss the budget of last year. Questions will be: Are the salaries of pastor, organist, sexton, and other members of the staff to be the same, or must there be increases or reductions? Will the same amount of fuel be used as last year, and is the price likely to be the same? Are there items on last year's budget which were for temporary emergencies, not to appear this year? Will emergency expenses for the coming year be beyond the expectancy for last year? The making of a budget requires hard work; there will be comparison, research, consultation with the pastor and other officials, and a close scrutiny of the program outlined for the coming year. A certain amount should be allowed for "miscellaneous expenses."

Once the committee decides on the expenditures on the basis of an irreducible minimum plus a safety margin for the expected expenses of the church, and has given due attention to what the church ought to be doing by inserting larger sums here and there and new appropriations, it will turn to the income which is to balance the expenses. The plate offerings will prove to be the largest source of revenue in the average church, aside from pledges; then there will be interest from invested funds for some churches, and regular gifts from organizations. All income, exclusive of pledges and loose offerings, will be deducted from the expense side of the budget, and the balance will show the minimum amount needed for the year.

A current expense budget should include such items as: salaries; pulpit supplies; pensions; parsonage, including general expense and repair; church building repairs and renovation; interest on mortgage; fuel, light, gas, and water; office expense, including printing, stationery, postage, supplies; telephone, advertising, dues, subscriptions, and church literature; music; church school, vacation and weekday school; woman's society, youth fellowship, other clubs and societies; insurance, bonds and custody accounts; contingencies.

Estimated income should include such items as, plate collection —loose offering; trust funds and rentals; men's fellowship or council, woman's society, and youth fellowship; church school, including Sunday, vacation and weekday school; other sources. The amount to be raised through pledges should balance the income with estimated expenditures. Sometimes there will be more than enough to do this.

It will be observed that this setup is in the transition period from the old type to the inclusive budget. Church school expenses and income are listed, but sometimes the Woman's Society expenses are handled by that group, and the balance is treated as a gift to the church. The Baptist Youth Fellowship, through the Fellowship Sharing Plan, should assume a portion of the budget of the church, both for current expenses and for missions and benevolences.

Another thing to note is that this is a tentative budget. This is as it should be, for the pledges have not been taken as yet. The budget committee will submit this estimate to the trustees or to the church for provisional approval and then turn it over to the Every Member Canvass committee. When the returns from pledge Sunday come in, the budget committee will revise downward or upward on the basis of the pledges and again submit the resulting budget to the church, this time for adoption. If the church does not approve of cuts which may be made to balance the budget, it may vote to adopt the original budget and balance it by an item listed as "deficit." This procedure is wise only if the church has a surplus of invested money upon which to draw, or if the outlook of the church for increased membership and attendance is cheerful enough to warrant "taking a chance," or going on in faith. A deficit budget is the responsibility of the church and trustees and not of the budget committee. Of course, a budget oversubscribed may be held at the "tentative" level. Then the balance can be voted out later.

8. *Financial Enlistment Committee.* In the area of church finance there are two pressing needs which are found in nearly every church. One is the need for a greater sense of Christian Stewardship on the part of individual members. The other is the very practical need for funds to meet the budget requirements of the church.

The Division of World Mission Support of the American Baptist Convention is charged with the responsibility "to develop a spirit of beneficence among the constituency." In fulfilling this responsibility its leaders and staff have sought not only to raise funds for the Baptist World Mission, but also to help local churches develop a greater sense of stewardship among their members and thus provide funds for the total ministry of the church. Baptists have been foremost in the development of tools for carrying out one of the most important projects in the life of the church, that of the annual financial enlistment. Each year under the leadership of a capable field staff and specially trained volunteers, instruction is made available to the pastor and financial leaders of every local church. Perhaps your church has sent representatives to training meetings. If not, take advantage of the next one to be held in your area. An inquiry at your state convention or city mission society office will give you the information you need about forthcoming training sessions.

For a number of years the emphasis was placed upon the 8-step Every Member Canvass as the vehicle for the annual financial enlistment. This is still a valid program, using tested methods and materials. A manual giving complete instructions, called *Steps to Greater Christian Service,* is available. If its instructions are followed closely, a local church will not only secure greater financial support but will find its spiritual tone improved as its people participate and share more devotedly.

Beginning in 1962, in response to many requests from pastors and lay leaders, a new emphasis was brought into the plans and materials. Known as the Tithing Enlistment Program, it makes use of the tested methods and excellent materials developed in the E.M.C., but places the emphasis upon tithing as the basis for the individual's Christian Commitment.

A Manual for Tithing Enlistment, giving detailed instructions, is available to every local church. New and attractive materials are produced each year and training in their use is also provided.

If the church utilizes one or both of these manuals, the necessity will be seen for an Every Member Canvass Committee, with each member having a special responsibility for conducting this annual enlistment program on whatever basis the church decides. The duties of the committee, chiefly, will be to plan for the enlistment, set up the special training committees for the teams which are to go out, arrange for the publicity materials and the pledge cards, conduct the enlistment on the day or week set aside, and carry through to completion this part of the church's work. The committee will have its task completed only when the enlistment is done insofar as possible, and the results are handed over to the budget committee, financial secretary, or whoever the church decides should make a record of the pledges received. (As has been said before, it is wise to keep this information confidential and the financial secretary usually is the one to see the pledges which have come in.)

If the church does not use the manuals mentioned, or any other guidance materials, the committee will need to do some very substantial work on its own in studying methods and ways and means of conducting this annual enlistment for funds for the program of the church. It is usually unwise, however, for a committee to go on its own, inasmuch as such helpful materials are available from the denominational offices.

FOR STUDY AND DISCUSSION

1. Analyze the spiritual quality of the office of trustee, remembering that the property of the church is all the result of gifts of dedicated money.

2. Compare the advantages and disadvantages of multiplying the financial offices in a church to give more people "something to do" as over against the efficiency of a simple organization.

3. Does it seem that a church operating under a balanced budget is depending more upon hard cash than faith in God? Should a church be businesslike?

4. Should the church consider a pledge legally binding, or ought it to be subject to cancellation at the request of the pledgee? Some years ago a church sued the maker of a pledge for non-payment. The man was well able to pay; was the church action right or wrong?

5. How should the Every Member Canvass Committee deal with members who say they are willing to give but are not willing to pledge a definite amount?

PROJECTS FOR CLASS REPORT

1. Make a chart showing the financial officers of your church, indicating the line of responsibility and listing the duties of each man or woman.

2. Two people may take opposite sides of the case for solicited pledges and be prepared to read their papers, pro and con.

3. Consider the method of financing in some churches which depends completely upon freewill offerings, because they find no reference to the Every Member Canvass or Enlistment in the New Testament. Do you agree or disagree with this reasoning?

CLASS PROJECT

1. Resolve the class into an Every Member Canvass committee, and work out the details for a canvass in the church.

2. Prepare a budget estimate. If different from the present budget, interpret the recommended changes.

BIBLIOGRAPHY

Manual—Percentage Giving Program, American Baptist Convention.

Every Member Canvass and Percentage Giving Program of the American Baptist Convention.

Manual—Explorations in Stewardship, American Baptist Convention.

Keech, William J., *The Life I Owe.*

CHAPTER V

The Work of Church School Officers

THERE WAS a time, the past tense is used optimistically, when there was a distinct division between "church" and "school." By "church" was meant the customary services of worship, and by "school" the Sunday hour preceding or following the morning service, or in the early afternoon, spent in studying the Bible and its meaning. Not only was there little correlation between the two, but often there was open rivalry. Many families would make a choice on Sunday between "church" and "school." Sunday school was the term used, and it was quite accurate for there was no thought of a school at any other time in the week. The last generation has seen a gradual and radical shift of opinion among leaders in Christian education.

The new interpretation is that the school of a church is much broader in scope and has too many functions to be restricted to Sunday. The church in the community has in its keeping the complete message of triumphant Christian living. The school of a church needs more time than one hour on Sunday to teach the contents of the Bible, and it needs time to teach the application of biblical content, reaching out to the home, the community, the nation, and the world. The church has something to teach a boy or girl, man or woman that will help him to make Christian decisions in every area of life: economic, political, social, moral, and spiritual. This chapter, then will deal with the work of leaders in the church school as they operate on a functional basis.

I. Divisions of the Church School

The size of a church largely will determine the number and extent of the educational activities that are possible and advisable. In a well-organized church school will be found the old-style Sunday school; Sunday evening groups, including Sunday morning church school, roughly approximate to the

66

children's groups, youth groups, young adult, and often adult fellowships (making up what is known as the Baptist Evening Fellowship) ; weekday church school; vacation church school; and miscellaneous activities, such as clubs and scouts.

II. General Leadership

The size and budget of a church will determine the type of leadership possible for the church school. But every church, no matter how small or large, needs to delegate the general authority for the church school to a board of education in order that the program may be correlated properly.

1. *The board of Christian education.* The advisability of having a board of Christian education will be discussed fully in Chapter VI. If a church has such a board, the supervision of the church school will devolve upon it.

2. *The pastor.* In small churches, it is possible that the pastor will be the only person who has had training and experience in Christian education methods. In this event, he will assume the responsibility for directing the program. In any case, the pastor will exercise his ex officio privileges in a way to insure an effective church school.

3. *The volunteer director of education.* A church that could not afford a paid director had among the membership a woman who was a "critic teacher" in the school system of a large city. In addition to her knowledge of up to date methods of secular education, she had attended a number of summer conferences on religious education and had earned both first and second series leadership certificates. It goes without saying that the church had in this member a volunteer director of Christian education of adequate capacity. Many churches are not so fortunate in personnel, but often there is a person who may be entrusted with the task under the guidance of the pastor.

4. *The paid director of Christian education.* A full-time director is to be desired, and a church large enough to need a director, but with limited funds, may be able to find a part-time director at a near-by seminary or training school. The method of selecting a director, and the major duties are discussed in Chapter I. An additional point to be made here is that the church should be informed as to the functions and responsibilities of this new, paid worker. Unless there is a clear under-

standing, the director may be imposed upon by members, and sometimes by the staff, who think that here is just another salaried staff member who may be asked to sing in the choir, do secretarial work, or play the piano for the woman's society. On the other hand, without a clear understanding of the duties of the director, some lay leaders may repel or ignore suggestions or recommendations coming from that source.

III. The Sunday Church School

Undoubtedly the Sunday morning session of the church school plays the major role in Christian education. Here all ages are represented in a traditionally accepted organization, planned with special emphasis on a systematic study of the Bible in order to become familiar with its contents and to apply its teachings to life today. Many of the pupils in this session of the school will be under the influence of the curriculum for many years. This is a choice opportunity for the building of Christian character and the development of leaders. The lion's share of the church appropriation for education may be invested profitably here, and the best leaders available should give their time to this work.

1. *General superintendent.*

(a) *The method of selection.* He is elected by the church, although the board of Christian education may have the privilege of suggesting a name to the nominating committee. The term of office is one year usually, with no limit on re-election, though some churches establish a limit of five consecutive years.

(b) *Qualifications* for this office are exacting. The chief requirements are: administrative ability, leadership ability, tact, sound judgment, familiarity with the newest church school methods, a passion for education, a spirit of unselfish co-operation, willingness, and ability to give much time to the job. These qualifications must be combined with a real personal Christian experience. In small communities, particularly, the superintendent is one whose influence is great. In all communities, he is watched and followed by the children and young people in his school.

(c) *Duties* of the superintendent are as many and as exacting as the qualifications.

(1) *Working under direction.* If the church school is to be an integral part of the total church program, the superintendent of the Sunday morning session cannot do his work independently of others. In a large church, he will have a board of Christian education and a director whose plans and programs will delimit his own work. In a smaller church, he will defer to the pastor as one having a more complete vision of the total church objective. The superintendent is one of a team of loyal people working toward the goals set for the year and rarely is he at the forefront in direction.

(2) *Administration.* The superintendent is the chief executive of his own sector of the educational work, the Sunday morning session of the church school. Under his leadership, there will be a staff of volunteer workers including, in a large school, an assistant superintendent, divisional superintendents for children, youth, adults, a secretary, a librarian, a pianist, and a corps of department superintendents, teachers, and substitute teachers. In a small school, he may have none to help except a few teachers. In any situation, he will be responsible for defining the tasks of his staff, and for helping each one to be busy at his own job. His will be the duty to provide all essential equipment at the time when it is needed. Equipment needed on Sunday morning includes blackboards, chalk and erasers, Bibles, quarterlies and other literature, pictures, visual education apparatus, and chairs.

The superintendent should arrange with his teachers that they notify him in advance of any expected absences, so he can arrange for substitute teachers to take the classes involved. He will make a quick check of the school on Sunday morning to catch any emergency absence. If a substitute teacher is not ready on short notice, a merger of two classes may have to be effected. In addition to these specific jobs of administration, everything else which adds to the efficient, smooth-functioning school will demand the attention of the superintendent. Many of the administrative jobs can be broken down among staff members; for instance, each teacher might be made responsible for checking her equipment before class time each week; but the final responsibility rests upon the superintendent.

(3) *Presiding officer.* Many small schools have a general assembly of all classes before or after the class period. Unless he has made other arrangements for the conduct of the assembly periods, the superintendent will preside. In large schools, there will be occasional general assemblies and other events at which the superintendent will preside. At business sessions of the school staff, at many workers' conferences, at special Christmas and other holiday events, the superintendent will be in charge or be responsible for delegating the task. He will represent the Sunday morning school on the board of Christian education, the advisory board, at church meetings and at interdenominational affairs. He will be, literally, the "voice" of the morning session.

(4) *Ex officio adviser.* The superintendent is an ex officio member of all school committees. He should be present at all important meetings, to keep himself informed and to add to the discussion by bringing in facts related to the whole program. Most of the important planning work

of the school will be done in committees and divisional group meetings and, because of this, the superintendent will be enabled to do much of his administrative work in an unobtrusive but effectual way.

(5) *Spiritual leader.* The superintendent will set the devotional pace of his staff by his undeviating insistence upon a brief worship period to open all staff meetings, by gathering the teachers and officers together before the Sunday session for quietness and prayer, and by making available to the members of his corps the best devotional materials. He will set the example in regular church attendance, also.

(6) *Research.* The superintendent will do well to continue his own leadership training by enrolling in administrative courses. His presence as a scholar or teacher in the annual leadership school will do more to bring his teachers than much urging. In addition to formal courses, he will read journals and books about his work, visit sessions of other church schools, and evaluate every denominational suggestion or plan. In the long run, a church school Sunday morning session will be as progressive as its general superintendent.

2. *An assistant superintendent* may be appointed to work with the general superintendent and represent him when he is absent. A small school may not need an assistant superintendent, while an exceptionally large school may require several. Even though the work does not warrant the election of an assistant in a small school, peculiar circumstances may make the office advisable. For instance: The present superintendent may have held office for many years, may be aging, may have announced his determination to relinquish the job at the end of the year. Under one or more of these conditions it is wise to "break in" a new man.

The assistant will be elected in the same manner as the superintendent, and the qualifications will be the same, except that more latitude may be allowed on the side of experience. The chosen person will gain his experience on the job.

The duties will depend largely on the personality of the superintendent. The assistant's job is to "assist," and he will do those things which his chief wishes to delegate to him. For one thing, the assistant usually makes the morning tour of the departments and classes to make sure that there are no unreported absences of workers. The superintendent may choose to give over to his assistant the task of procuring the necessary supplies. And, of course, the assistant will take the helm whenever the superintendent is absent.

3. *Secretary.* Even in small schools a secretary is important.

He usually is appointed by the general superintendent with the approval of the board of Christian education.

His primary task is to keep the records. There will be a classbook, or set of attendance cards, for each class. These must be distributed on Sunday morning and collected after the attendance has been marked. From these records, the secretary will take off a summary of the number of teachers, officers, and pupils present, the amount of the offering, and any other details of interest to the school. Then the report will be given to the superintendent who may wish to make some announcement about it before the session closes, or the information may be put on an attendance board.

The secretary's records are valuable, too, when graphs are made, to show the trends in attendance and to compare with former years. Often a comparative graph will show up a weak spot which needs special attention.

In addition to being the record-keeper, the secretary may take the minutes of workers' conferences and other business gatherings of the school staff. A good secretary will make, or cause to be made, transcripts of the minutes for mailing to all of the staff members. Frequently, also, there will be letters to write, such as notifying committee members of their appointment.

4. *Librarian.* In small schools, this office may be combined with that of secretary, but the following duties will fall upon the librarian. The librarian will make up the quarterly, or monthly, order for supplies in co-operation with the superintendent. There will be the need for quarterlies, leaflets, workbooks, pictures, story papers, teacher's manuals, and many other items. After the arrival of the supplies, the librarian will be responsible for delivering them to the teachers and officers, and for keeping the surplus materials ready in the event of new enrollments or mislaid books. The efficiency with which the librarian performs his task will directly affect the efficiency of the school. Teachers, forced to improvise for even one Sunday without the aid of the materials for that day, will be handicapped for the entire quarter. And a new pupil who must wait for weeks for his own book and work materials may be lost to the school.

In schools maintaining a workers' library and a library available to pupils, the librarian will be responsible for keeping books in good condition, for keeping records of withdrawals and return, for writing up a catalogue of the books owned, for ordering new books when authorized by the minutes of staff meetings.

5. *Division superintendents.* In churches with a small membership and with small schools, it is entirely possible that a gifted person will need to teach as well as serve in the capacity of division superintendent. It is well, however, to give this title and responsibility to someone in the division even though he or she may be one of two or three teachers in that age group. The general superintendent is "general," and he needs someone in each of the three divisions to be specialists.

(*a*) *Superintendent of children's work.* This official will be appointed by the board of Christian education as will the other division superintendents in a church having a board; otherwise the general superintendent will present the name of his choice to the staff for ratification.

The superintendent in the children's division will have oversight of all work for ages one to eleven—nursery through juniors. In a fully departmentalized school, this will mean that the superintendent has four or possibly five departments under his or her supervision: nursery, kindergarten, primary, middlers (in some churches), and junior. There will be one or more classes in each department.

The duties of this superintendent will be much the same as those of the general superintendent except that they will be confined to the children's division. Planned meetings with the children's staff will be held regularly, equipment will be checked frequently, assemblies or departmental worship periods will be arranged, teachers will be encouraged to attend leadership training schools and conferences, arrangements for substitutes will be cleared with the general superintendent, the needs and progress of the division will be presented at general staff meetings and, by permission of the general superintendent, before the board of Christian education or the church. The superintendent will give thought to the best use of the space available to the division. The superintendent will be on the children's work staff in churches having a special supervisor for all children's work. This is the person who should carry the convention children's program to the children's workers.

(*b*) *Superintendent of youth work.* The age range in the youth division is from twelve to twenty-five. Many churches will find it hard to hold to this ideal division, for after eighteen many of the young people drift into young adult activities, or even into adult classes. This is due to the varying degree of maturity evident, to the choice between industry and school, and, sometimes, to early marriages. However, the superintendent in this division will do his or her best to plan activities for youth within this age range.

In the departmentalized school, this superintendent has three departments to cultivate: junior high, senior high, and young people with one or more classes in each. In addition, in churches having a Sunday evening session of the church school, he may have work in the fellowship groups.

His duties will be similar to the superintendent of children's work, except that in the youth field greater provision must be made for social and recreational events during the week as direct adjuncts to the Sunday classes, with youth taking a larger share in formulating and carrying out the plans.

(c) *Superintendent of adult work.* The superintendent in this division will be responsible on Sunday mornings for adults, age twenty-five and up. In many churches this is the smallest area of work, although it has, often, the greatest potential value.

There will be three departments of work: Young adult, adult, and home department. In a small church, there may be but one class and a home department, although larger churches may have many classes. If at all possible, the superintendent of this division will divide the young adults and adults into separate classes.

For the duties, we refer again to the section on the superintendent of children's work. In addition, the adult superintendent may find that he is responsible for discussion groups in the young adult field, and he will work in co-operation with the workers in the nursery and home departments in order to keep the young adults in touch with the church during the days of "baby-sitter" problems.

IV. *The Baptist Evening Fellowship*

The Baptist Evening Fellowship may meet on Sunday evening or on any other evening during the week, but whenever it meets it is a logical and integral part of the work of the church school.

In brief, the Baptist Evening Fellowship is a fully graded evening program which provides that church members or attendants may come by families, bringing even their youngest children with them, to enjoy planned experiences for all ages. The development of a Baptist Evening Fellowship will provide a new opportunity for ministering to the deepest needs of persons by involving them in small fellowship groups, for Bible study, prayer, fellowship, and training.

1. *Auspices of the board of Christian education.* The Baptist Evening Fellowship is a part of the church's educational program, and therefore is administered by the Board, or committee, of Christian Education. This Board will accept the same responsibility for the Baptist Evening Fellowship that it exercises in regard to the Sunday morning church school and other phases of the educational program.

2. *The co-ordinator.* A co-ordinator, elected annually by the Board of Christian Education, should function in relationship to the Baptist Evening Fellowship in much the same way that the General Superintendent serves the Sunday church school. The co-ordinator should exercise the following responsibilities:

(a) Be thoroughly familiar with the Baptist Evening Fellowship Program and be able to interpret it to others.

(b) Call meetings for program planning. There will need to be certain designated times for planning the program of the fellowship. These will include an extended planning period once a year for developing long range program, and regular quarterly checkup meetings. These meetings should be attended by the three age group chairmen, the chairman of the Board of Christian Education, the pastor, and the leaders of all departmental fellowship programs.

(c) Arrange for someone to preside at general sessions of the Baptist Evening Fellowship, particularly the TOGETHER TIME experiences.

(d) Co-ordinate the entire program and work in close co-operation with the age group chairmen.

(e) Deal with emergency problems, such as the unexpected absence of a leader. The co-ordinator will be the trouble shooter of the program.

(f) Help to promote recruitment and regular attendance of members.

(g) Serve as an ex-officio member of the Board of Christian Education. In this capacity the co-ordinator will be able to integrate the program and leadership of the Baptist Evening Fellowship with the total church program.

In co-operation with the Board of Christian Education, the co-ordinator will be responsible for enlisting whatever help is needed for the fellowship meetings. This will depend largely upon the size of the church and the potential attendance at the evening meetings. In some churches it may not be possible to maintain departments for all ages, and in some churches one department may be much larger than any other. These things will determine the required number of division or departmental helpers and teachers. Perhaps the word "teacher" is not too well taken, for the Evening Fellowship is planned around small intimate groups, and even at the lower age levels there is provision for constant participation of all people involved.

3. *Youth program and adviser.* With or without a full Evening Fellowship program, there should be definite provision for the Youth Fellowship program. The Sunday morning youth department superintendent should co-operate with the evening adviser. The fellowship activities then would include both the Sunday morning church school and the Evening Fellowship; for Junior High, 12 to 14; Senior High, 15 to 17; and young people, 18 to 25. Although the same leaders and counselors may not be at both Sunday sessions for youth, every effort should be made to build the activities into one complete experience.

The adult leader of youth may be known as the Adviser. This adviser will utilize the leadership of the young people; he will encourage and control presentation of the work by the youth members. He will guide youth to participate in worship and discussion in preference to having an adult direct the study of some text. He will sit in on all planning sessions for social events, and exercise guidance if youthful exuberance overflows. And he will be present at all social functions. He will be called upon to give reports of his work to the Board of Christian Education, and possibly to the church.

4. *Schools of Missions and Schools of Evangelism,* as encouraged by the denomination, can be easily integrated into a Baptist Evening Fellowship. If there is no Baptist Evening Fellowship in the church these activities and Schools of Christian Living

may be presented periodically under the auspices of a director of the schools or some member of the Board of Christian Education to whom this responsibility may be assigned. If the schools are conducted according to age groupings, then the representatives on the Board of Christian Education responsible for the various age groups will also be involved in this program.

V. Weekday Church School

In spite of some uncertainty about this phase of church school work at the present time, the work is going forward in many localities and adds up to a sizable block of the total church school work.

Inasmuch as weekday work is largely an interdenominational and community affair, no one church has the responsibility or privilege of naming the director. In community efforts, this official is elected at a gathering of representatives of all the churches involved. The group will include pastors, general superintendents, the chairman of the board of Christian education from each church, and a number of delegates-at-large. The meeting of this elective assembly comes in March or April usually, and plans are made for the next school year. The director, an assistant director, a secretary, and a treasurer may be elected. Churches are assessed according to the number of children from their membership who are involved, and donations are welcomed from civic and church organizations as well as from individuals.

The elected director and his staff will plan the school in accordance with the laws and precedents of the community. The possibilities are:

(a) *Released classes.* In this setup the classes leave the public school buildings and go to the churches or other places provided by the weekday staff. It is the responsibility of the director of the school to furnish escorts to and from the public school building. At busy corners the local police may be utilized by arrangement with the town authorities, but the main job will be done by volunteers from the churches. The classes are permitted to be absent from public school for one hour or one period.

(*b*) *After school time.* This is a rare setup, because the children are no longer under the public school authority and will not be marked absent on the records for failure to attend the class in religion. If the co-operation of the parents and the program are on a high level, this method works. Escorts meet the children at the public school at dismissal time and conduct them to the place of instruction.

Under released class methods, the compulsion on the child to attend weekday school is dependent upon the parents. At the beginning of the school year, the public school teacher sends home to the parents of the children in her class a slip of paper which is to be signed with the designation as to whether or not the parents wish the child to attend the classes in religion and under which faith group, Protestant, Catholic, Jewish. With this slip goes a mimeographed or printed sheet describing the weekday work. The slips and sheets are provided by the weekday association.

When the hour arrives for the released time, four divisions are made in the class: one goes to the Protestant place of instruction, one to the Catholic, one to the Jewish, and the fourth continues public school work, inasmuch as the parents have chosen to keep their children out of the religious classes.

The director and his staff must select teachers and decide upon the curriculum for the year. Under released time or class arrangements, the municipality demands that the teachers measure up to the same standards required of the public school instructors. They will be volunteers or paid according to the local system. The courses will be as closely integrated with the public school work as possible.

Weekday schools rarely start their work below the fourth grade or go beyond junior high level. This varies, of course, with each community.

Commencement exercises are planned by the weekday staff. Children having completed the entire course of study will be awarded a certificate. Merit awards for good work are frequently given.

The weekday teachers grade the pupils as carefully as public school teachers, and they are authorized to demand the same standard of discipline. The grades are sometimes passed on to the public school teachers to go on the report card; otherwise the weekday teachers send the parents a separate report.

(c) *Shared time.* A full study is being made of a program to be called Shared Time, which in brief will mean that parochial school students will be using public school facilities at certain times during the school day. This will mean, in all likelihood, that anything that has to do with religion or ethics will be the responsibility of the various religious bodies; that is to say that the Catholics will take their children back to their parochial school buildings for those subjects; the Jewish children will go to the synagogues; and the Protestant children will go to a church, or churches, in the community, according to the plans which the Protestant leaders set up. If this plan materializes, the local church will find a need for co-operating in a community enterprise much on the order of the present program for a Released Time Session, except that the subjects may be more diverse and more of a general nature.

VI. Vacation Church School

The vacation church school is a summer session distinctly and may be from one to six weeks in length. Co-operative community schools of denominational or interdenominational nature are growing in popularity due to the encouraging impetus of a large work and the difficulty of assembling a staff for each church.

A vacation church school staff is appointed or elected in the manner of the weekday staff if the work is community-wide. If a single church plans its own school, the staff will be gathered as in the Sunday morning session of the church school. A general superintendent or director, his assistant, departmental supervisors, teachers, a secretary, a treasurer, a pianist, and specialists in activities will be needed.

Children will be invited to attend by means of publicity in the Sunday morning sessions in the churches, by posters and announcements in the public schools if this is permitted, by newspaper space, and by mail. An advance registration is advisable in order to guide the staff in allotting space and equipment to the various classes, and as a gauge for ordering supplies.

The curriculum of a local school is easily arranged, due to

the exact planning of the denominational boards; a community school requires many staff meetings to select the best from the various agencies while avoiding sectarian bias.

The superintendent will finance the school according to the instructions of those who have appointed him. The entire sum required may come from church treasuries, some may come in response to a plea for funds made in the churches, some may come from registration fees or offerings in the school itself. The children are required, in some instances, to pay for their more expensive handwork materials. In some communities the children cannot be expected to share in the expense.

The sessions of a vacation school extend, customarily, from nine o'clock until noon, Monday through Friday. The afternoons are free except for picnics or other outings. The commencement and closing exhibition of handwork frequently is held in the evening in order to draw in as many parents as possible.

VII. Summer Opportunities

In addition to the divisions of the church school discussed in this chapter, there are summer opportunities. Conferences, camps, retreats, day camps, picnics, occasional hikes, playground work, nature study, community service projects, give the board of Christian education and other leaders openings for church school work which may well contribute to the growth of Christian character and knowledge.

FOR STUDY AND DISCUSSION

1. Compare the meanings of "Sunday school," and "church school." If a church has no other teaching activity beyond the Sunday morning session, may that organization be termed a "church school"?

2. "The Little Red Schoolhouse" often had eight grades in one room with one teacher. Many small churches find themselves in much the same situation with the exception that several teachers are available. Discuss ways and means of making one small room into a departmentalized Sunday morning session.

3. In the class will be found members who have held many of the offices described in this chapter. They may compare the material in the chapter with their own official experience. Hand findings to the senior church school officer.

4. Many churches conduct a nursery during morning worship for the convenience of mothers who must bring babies or very young children. Can this kind of nursery be linked up to the church school?

5. Has this chapter exhausted the possibilities of a church school, or are there other expressions of its work unmentioned?

PROJECTS FOR CLASS REPORT

1. Make a chart of all activities in your own church which fall under the general classification of church school, showing the approximate number of persons touched by each organization.

2. Prepare a pro or con statement on the value of a weekday school, depending upon released time or in class training, in the light of recent church-state arguments.

3. Procure a vacation church school text and a Sunday morning session text for the same grade. Discuss the list of the chief differences in approach and content.

CLASS PROJECT

Prepare a bibliography of helpful books in the field of church school work and make it available to the churches represented.

Write to Audio-Visual Department, Valley Forge, Pa., for a catalog of slide sets available on church school planning and leadership. Arrange to show some to the class.

BIBLIOGRAPHY

Cober, Kenneth L., *Baptist Evening Fellowship Manual.*

Gilbert, Clarence L., *The Board of Christian Education at Work.*

Jones, Idris W., *The Superintendent Plans His Work.*

CHAPTER VI

The Work of the Board of Christian Education

THE GROWTH AND OUTREACH of the Christian church has been much like that of a great university. Many universities can trace their origin to an "academy," an elementary type of school designed to lay the foundation for cultured living. The academy grew into a college equipped and staffed to teach the "arts." One by one, other colleges were staffed to specialize in law, medicine, music, and other fields. The result—a university. As the needs of the nation became more diverse, the school kept pace in offering means of preparation for a more complex civilization. And so it is with the church.

At first, the apostles were all-sufficient to preach, teach, and dispense alms. The alms giving and visiting called forth the officers now known as deacons. Later, when churches became possessed of buildings and funds, men now known as trustees became indispensable. Unfortunately, many churches have felt that there has been no needed advance in organization since the creation of a board of trustees. The tremendous educational responsibilities too frequently have been loaded onto a church annex called the "Sunday school." The truth is that the educational function of the church today extends into areas untouched by the Sunday school. The church can and should be a great "University of Christian Living." To cope with these three great opportunities of the church, forward-looking congregations have at least three boards on a par with one another: the board of deacons, the board of trustees, and the board of Christian education. This chapter will deal with the third, the board of Christian education, which is in every way as important to the life of a church as are the others.

The Board of Christian Education

A board of Christian education is a group of men and women selected by a church for the purpose of unifying all of

81

the Christian education organizations, activities, and efforts of the local church, to create and promote essential activities hitherto omitted, and to co-ordinate all similar or duplicate efforts. This definition will gain in meaning as the duties of the board are explored.

1. *How organized.* A church without a board of Christian education, and with no provision made for one in the constitution, will need to prepare and submit for adoption a by-law similar to the sample to be found in *The Board of Christian Education at Work,* a pamphlet published by the Board of Education and Publication of the American Baptist Convention. This sample rarely will suit the local situation without some changes, but it is an excellent guide.

2. *How elected.* The by-law will provide for election procedures, but the most efficient provision has proved to be that which calls for the election of one-third of the board annually. The regular nominating committee of the church will bring in these names with others on the slate. A board of three persons will be rotated so that one member is elected each year, a board of six will need two new members each year. (Refer to the paragraph on the election of deacons in Chapter III.) If the members of the board are made ineligible for re-election until after the lapse of a year, a rotating board will be the result.

3. *The Membership.* The pastor of the church, the director of Christian education, where there is one, and the general superintendent of the Sunday church school should be ex officio members of the board. All other members will be elected by the church. The board should be made up of sufficient persons to give adequate attention to all that is included in the church's total educational program, including work with children, youth, and adults.

The size of the board depends largely upon local conditions and will be determined primarily by the size of the church. A church of one hundred members or less should have a board of three, a church of two to four hundred needs six, and a church of five hundred or over may require nine. By including ex officio committee members from outside the personnel of the board, the largest church need not go beyond nine elected members. The elected members are not to be selected on the basis of their activity in some educational organization of the church, such as Sunday church school, Baptist Youth Fellowship, Girl Scouts, inasmuch as this would reduce the board to a council of related activities. Nor should the board be too heavily loaded with people whose chief efforts have been in the Sunday church school. Perhaps the following qualifications will give point to the foregoing statements:

4. *Qualifications of members.* Christian character is the standard of qualification for members of a board of Christian education. This is true of deacons and trustees, and certainly it is essential in work that will determine much of the Christian growth in grace of many members of a church. With all charity, the nominating committee needs to consider the character of a candidate from the basis of personal religious experience expressed through activity as a church member.

It is possible, however, for a person to be admirable in experience and activity and yet to confine that activity to one particular project. This one should be left to his favorite project, for his interests are not broad enough for this board. A board member should have wide interests in the many-sided work of his church.

Even so we have not found the "ideal" board member. Added to the two qualifications noted, the ideal member will be a man or woman of open mind and eagerness to learn, with a capacity for growth. In no other field are methods and resources changing so rapidly as in the field of education. A board member needs to be one who is willing to investigate new material and every new approach. He should be familiar with improved methods of education and, if possible, have some experience in the field of education.

Of course, the average church will not be able to find enough "ideal" members available even for a small board. The nominating committee must approximate the ideal and counter the weakness of one member with the strength of another so that the board will always have represented (1) deep personal religious experience, (2) wide interests, (3) possibilities for mental and spiritual growth, and if possible, (4) experience with the best educational procedures.

5. *Organization.* Unless the church has designated the officers of the board, an organizational meeting should be held soon after the church election to select the chairman and secretary. At this meeting, preliminary work can be done on set-

ting up committees and assigning responsibility to members of the board. Where the board is large enough for specialized work, the organization should provide for a Chairman of Children's Work, a Chairman of Youth Work, a Chairman of Adult Work, a Chairman of Leadership Education, and a Chairman of Missionary and Stewardship Education. Each of these chairmen will have as his working committee a small group of others involved in the respective activity. It cannot be stressed too strongly that the Board must operate functionally. Because there is frequent misunderstanding concerning the relationship of ex officio members, it may be well to set down some guiding principles. First, let it be clear that an ex officio member is one who is a member of the board by virtue of the office he holds. According to Robert's *Rules of Order,* an ex officio member has full privileges of membership, including the right to vote on all matters coming before the board and should be used on subcommittees of the board. An ex officio member, however, will not be counted in determining a quorum.

6. *Duties.* The tasks of the board criss-cross and intertwine, but for the sake of classification they may be looked at under five general heads: administration, leadership, curriculum, outreach, and budget.

(a) Administration

(1) *Survey.* Only in a new church could a board hope to start from scratch. In the church will be classes, groups, fellowships, clubs, programs which have been in existence for some time. These cannot be dissolved at the wave of a wand in order to give the board a free hand, nor would it be wise to try it. The first task of a new board is to make a complete survey of the total educational program of the church at the moment. With the results of this survey before it, the board can compare the present setup with the program that it believes will be most efficient and best serve the needs of the church. The old must be fitted into the new. Just as though a cutout picture were placed over an outline sketched on a drawing board, the old will overlap in some spots and fail to reach the line in others. If the board is convinced that its program is undeniably better than the program, or lack of program, found in the church, it must have the courage to make the necessary adjustments. Some activities will call for elimination, others for expansion; voids here and there must be filled with new activities. It goes without saying that tact is the key word; arbitrariness is disastrous. No activity of a worthwhile character must be done away unless the values and the leadership personnel are conserved and the membership transferred to other classes or activities. The work of the board is creative, not destructive. However, if it comes to an issue between a distorted program and "hurt feelings,"

it sometimes is better to risk the hurt feelings.

(2) *Adoption of standards.* The board must settle within itself the results it expects from Christian education and map out objectives for the local church. If the program of the board seems good enough to present to the church as a "must," the church is entitled to know the objectives or goals toward which the program is moving. Every activity must have a purpose, every plan a reason. An example of this is found in the "Achievement Plan" set up for Baptist Sunday church schools. The plan has ten objectives: a *church* school, a *Bible* school, a *Baptist* school, an *evangelistic* school, a *missionary* school, a *growing* school, a *graded* school, a *planned* school, a *leader-trained* school, a *churchgoing* school. The activities of the Sunday church school are planned to move toward these goals.

The board will need to set up long-range and annual goals in all areas of its work, not only for the Sunday church school but for every phase of education. Help in this task will be found in *The Board of Christian Education at Work*, a pamphlet published by the Board of Education and Publication of the American Baptist Convention. It is important for the board to consult with every organization in the church in order that there may be understanding and close co-operation in the church's activities.

(3) *Housing.* The board is responsible for planning the use of the building, or buildings, available. A small church may have the auditorium and one or two small rooms, while a large church may boast many classrooms. The board must begin work with what is at hand and adapt the program and time schedule to the facilities. Judicious use of screens, movable partitions, curtains, and sound-deadening materials helps greatly. Cleanness is possible even in the most cramped quarters. Proper equipment often transforms a drab space into workable quarters. And equipment is a possibility, the cost of simple things is not prohibitive; much can be made by interested members, some can be solicited. The board should visit other schools to see how they arrange their schedule and equipment. Sometimes if a church is inadequate, the parsonage may house some classes. The board should see that the children have the best space and equipment.

(4) *The budget.*

   (a) *Preparation.* Although a church may not have a unified budget, it may include a budgetary allowance for educational purposes, or it may be persuaded to include such an item if the board will explain the advantages to the finance committee. As a matter of fact, a church which elects a board of Christian education must realize that the board cannot operate without funds. In ample time, before the organization of the church budget, the board should prepare its budget, itemized to show the recommended expenditures for each department of the work, such as Sunday church school and Youth Fellowship, together with the probable receipts. When the budget is completed it will be given to the chairman of the finance or budget committee of the church.

   (b) *Administration.* All revenues from the activities within the educational program which are not for special purposes should be turned over to the church treasurer. The responsibility for expending the budgeted money will be on the board. Bills for all authorized expenditures and authorization for special items should be handed to the church treasurer who will keep a separate accounting of the board's receipts and expenditures and provide a periodic statement to the board. Missionary offerings that are received through the church school activities should be turned over to the benevolence treasurer or to the general church treasurer, earmarked for the mission program. All special offerings of the church school should be handled by the treasurer for the designated purposes.

(5) *Miscellaneous.* At regular monthly meetings the board will continue its survey of progress and of new methods and materials. Reports will be made to the church as often as required, and a detailed report will be prepared for the annual meeting of the church.

(b) Leadership

(1) *Selection of leaders.* The board has the power to appoint all workers in the Sunday church school, vacation church school, and week-day church school, with the exception of the general superintendent of the Sunday church school. Departmental superintendents, secretaries, teachers, and assistant teachers will receive their appointment from the board. At the annual meeting of the church, the board may nominate a general superintendent of the Sunday church school, but the election will be by the church, and additional nominations may be made from the floor.

(2) *Training of leaders.* The board will arrange leadership training facilities to continue throughout the year. Standard leadership courses should be offered during church school time, before midweek meetings, and in special leadership schools in the community. Workers' conferences are important for general training, a library of selected books should be maintained, and opportunities should be afforded for attendance at camps, workshops, and laboratories beyond the community.

(3) *Encouragement of leaders.* The board will plan services of dedication for leaders, annual receptions, and special programs of recognition.

(4) *Search for leaders.* The ideal educational program is one which includes a plan for constant recruitment of potential leaders. The board will be on the lookout for promising people to be trained for immediate tasks or to be held in reserve for emergencies.

(c) Curriculum

It is logical that the board should select the basic materials to be used by teachers and other leaders in the educational program, inasmuch as the various activities are purposely inter-related. For instance, if the individual workers, or even the department heads in the church school, were given the privilege of selecting and using materials of their own choice, confusion would result. The curriculum provides for progression of experience from the small child to the adult. A unit omitted means some experiences lost. In the average person, Christian growth follows a plan, and the church school curriculum is developed to fit that plan. Special days and weeks, and various educational emphases in the general church program, will receive adequate attention and proper support. Of course, the board will consult with the workers involved and give them a vision of the whole scope of the curriculum.

(d) Outreach

(1) *To the unreached.* The educational program of the church will be planned by the board not only as an instrument for polishing and repolishing the gemlike lives under its ministration, but as an open and inviting door to draw in the outsiders from beyond the church portal. Indeed, the most vital part of the program will be the training of all age groups for sturdy witnessing to the saving power of the Christian message. The board of Christian education in a Baptist church has available the splendid programs of Winning the Children for Christ, Church School Enlargement program, Home Visitation Evangelism, New Friends for Christ. A wise board will include at least one of these special emphases in each year's plan.

(2) *To church families and homes.* The relationship between the homes of church families and the church and its program will be strengthened by the board. By emphasis on the development of the Christian home, by materials made available to parents and children, by demonstrations of home worship, by the fostering of home recreation, by panel discussions on the Christian family, by parents' night, and in other ways, the board will try to bring about a growing sense of unity between home and church. These homes are outposts of the educational program of the church.

(3) *Into the community.* The board will touch the geographical community of the church by co-operating with other churches and agencies through educational projects leading to the improvement of conditions and influences in the community. Separately, or with other churches, recreational facilities, vacation church schools, and perhaps weekday church schools will be sponsored by the board.

The denominational community of the church, which to Baptist churches is the American Baptist Convention, will be related to the work of the board as it promotes missionary education, stewardship, and an educational program leading to financial support and to action on convention projects; and the board will receive from the denomination the benefit of expert planning and leadership.

The interdenominational community concerns the board, too. Interdenominational participation in conferences, study groups, leadership schools, and institutes will become part of the responsibility of the board.

In interdenominational ways the board can train the membership to express the will of the church in Christian social action. In preparation for community and world relationships the representative of missionary education will be able to provide leadership and recommend curricular materials.

(e) The program

An adequate program of Christian education in the local church includes work with children, youth, and adults. The Sunday church school, vacation church school, and weekday church school are three of the most important organizations in the program. The youth fellowship functionally cuts across the organizational units, Sunday church school, Sunday evening group and weekday activities. Major educational emphases that touch the life of the whole church, such as missionary education, leadership education, stewardship education, student counseling, camping, family life are related elements of this program of Christian education. In other words, the board of Christian education should be responsible for planning and directing the total educational program of the church.

There are, of course, many ways in which the board membership may organize for effective work. Probably the most common is to recognize the major areas of work for which the board is responsible and organize about them. It is rather commonly agreed that these areas are: children's work, youth work, adult work, missionary education, leadership education, student counseling, and weekday church school and summer activities. In some churches, the organization includes emphasis on Christian family life, stewardship education, audiovisual education, home-church relations, and the like. In still other churches, there is an inclination to organize exclusively on what is called the "age-group basis," recognizing the fact that the entire program is designed to minister to children, youth, and adults.

It is important to reiterate that all members of the board of Christian education need to become conversant with the total educational work of the church. It will soon be discovered, however, that there is value in having each member assume particular responsibility for one or more phases of the program. Thus, definite responsibility should be accepted for children's work, youth work, adult work, missionary and stewardship education, and possibly other important phases of Christian education such as leadership education. In the case of a small board membership, such as will be necessary in a small church, some of the members will need to assume responsibility for more than one phase of the work. Whatever its size, and however its membership may be organized for work, the board of Christian education should be responsible for the organization, administration, and supervision of the entire educational program of the church.

Some have said that a church having 150 members or less does not need a board of Christian education. Others insist that the limited leadership available in a smaller church makes a board of Christian education a practical impossibility. Experience, however, points to the contrary, for in many churches of less than one hundred members there are effective boards of Christian education. Such boards usually operate with three elected members and two, or possibly three, ex officio members. The work is distributed among them, and, as in larger churches, others are drawn into the work of committees. The board itself will do many things while sitting as a committee-of-the-whole.

(f) *Summary*

Some practical suggestions for a board of any size are:

(1) Hold regular meetings, monthly if possible. Review what is being accomplished, and plan for the weeks and months ahead.

(2) Keep the church informed about what the board is doing.

(3) Obtain and study very carefully the handbook on *The Board of Christian Education at Work*. This carries the most helpful kind of suggestions for the use of the board in planning its annual program for the church. This handbook may be procured from the state or city director of Christian education, or from the Department of Church School Administration, Valley Forge, Pennsylvania.

(4) Select a limited number of definite goals for the year's work. Interpret them to the church, and keep them before the people.

(5) Remember these four basic principles of good board work:
Plan the program carefully.
Make certain that there is adequate leadership available.
Be sure the program is carried through.
Keep everlastingly at the business of evaluating what is done.

FOR STUDY AND DISCUSSION

1. If the church has no board of Christian education, compare the efficiency of the present program with the possibilities outlined in this chapter.

2. Work out a reasonable budget to be earmarked for Christian education of the church. How large a proportion would this be?

3. The chapter suggests that the work of the board of Christian education is on a par with that of the boards of deacons and trustees. Discuss the validity of this statement.

4. In a church the size of yours, what would be the most practical method of organizing the membership of a board of Christian education?

5. In the light of the discussion in this chapter, are there apparent gaps in the program of Christian education in your church?

PROJECTS FOR CLASS REPORT

1. Make a survey of the Christian education activities in your church, and list the number of different leaders in each activity.

2. If your church has a board of Christian education, interview the chairman and make a report of the work which is now being done.

CLASS PROJECT

Obtain for each member of the class a copy of *The Board of Christian Education at Work*. Assign each one of the areas to one or more members of the group, depending on the size of the class. Allow time for preparation, then resolve the class into a meeting of a board of Christian education and listen to the plans of the various chairmen as they outline the work for a year.

BIBLIOGRAPHY

Blankenship, Lois, *Our Church Plans for Children.*

Cummings, Oliver deW., *Christian Education in the Local Church.*

Evans, David M., *Shaping the Church's Ministry with Youth.*

Fidler, James E., *Our Church Plans for Leadership Education.*

Fordham, Forrest B., *Our Church Plans for Youth.*

Gilbert, Clarence L., *The Board of Christian Education at Work.*

Hanson, Joseph J., *Our Church Plans for Adults.*

Keech, William J., *Our Church Plans for Missionary and Stewardship Education.*